A Traveler's Advisory

Stories of God's Grace Along the Way

MARCIA LEE LAYCOCK

ISBN:
ISBN-13: 978-1512175097
ISBN-10: 1512175099

Box 637 Blackfalds

Alberta Canada

T0M 0J0

smallpond@telus.net

SmallPondPress.com

CONTENTS

An Irish Blessing for Travelers

May the blessings of light be upon you,

Light without and light within,

And in all your comings and goings,

May you ever have a kindly greeting

From them you meet along the road.

1 IN THE AIR

A Child's Absolute Trust

I was getting tired of standing. The long line winding its way to the airport's check-in counter seemed to be at a virtual stand-still. A few feet away from us, a young couple contended with a toddler. As their portion of the line moved forward, they soon stood beside us, separated only by the long strap marking the snaking path. The boy squirmed continually in his mother's arms. Finally her husband leaned over and took the child, but he was no more content in his father's arms. You could see the parents were exasperated.

My husband noticed. He made a face at the little boy and soon had his undivided attention. At first the child just stared. Then he grinned. Then he started to laugh.

Then, quite suddenly, that little boy flung himself into Spence's arms. No-one was more surprised than my husband, but he caught him and playfully talked to him, checking the expression on the father's face to make sure it was okay with him. The young man was obviously cautious, but relieved to no longer have a wiggling toddler in his arms. We chatted with the parents, acknowledging how hard it must be to hang on to such an active little boy. When the line started moving again, Spence handed the youngster back to his dad.

As we waited for our turn at the counter, I thought about the total, absolute trust that little boy had shown. Without hesitation he had flung himself into my husband's arms. I thought of the many books I had read about totally abandoning ourselves to God. I had just seen a picture of what it looked like and I realized how rarely I had ever done it. We adults have something to learn from the innocence and trust of little children. Perhaps that's what Jesus meant when He said that unless we come as little children, we cannot enter the kingdom of heaven (Matthew 18:3).

Absolute trust is hard for we who insist on control. We don't want to walk blindly into a situation. We want to know what to expect. We want to be prepared. Worldly wisdom dictates that those who do not take steps to control their lives are unwise at best, fools at worst. But listen to the writer of Proverbs 19:21 –

"Many are the plans in a man's heart, but it is the Lord's purpose that prevails." Putting your life, your whole life, into God's hands is not unwise. Trusting God is not foolish. All the schemes and plans we make will end in a pile of dust, like the tower of Babel, unless they are part of God's plan for our lives.

   Throw yourself into His arms. He knows what you need, what is best for you, and where you will be fulfilled and content. Trust Him.

****

Thoughts From 35,000 Feet

Sitting in a small seat thousands of feet above the earth, gives one an interesting perspective. It gives me a sense of being on the edge of something. Possibilities flit through my mind as I peer through the clouds.

   In that space of time there are, realistically, many possibilities. It's possible the plane might crash - unlikely, but possible - or I could be in a car accident far from home. It's possible I might never see my family again, or not have the mental capacity to recognize them when I do. It's possible that my life could be totally different by the time I return home. It's quite amazing how morbid my thoughts will run at 35,000 feet! Perhaps I've been watching too much T.V. Or perhaps, I'm just recognizing reality. We are all, in reality, on the edge of change.

Perhaps that's why I begin to ponder my earthly relationships. I get the urge to write letters, to say things I should take the time to say every day. Words like, "I love you," or "I was wrong, forgive me," or "your friendship means a lot," or those two simple words, "thank you." Spending several captive hours in an airplane forces me to slow down and recognize there are people in my life who should be cherished. Somehow thinking about them gives me new energy.

Over the past few months I've been to several women's retreats, both as an attendee and as a speaker. Those times away forced me to take the time to ponder a spiritual relationship, with my Almighty Father. There too, I recognized my failure to communicate - all the times I didn't say the thank-you's, or give the praise, or just acknowledge His presence. The retreats caused me to pause and focus on that relationship. They gave me time to think about how I should be cherishing God, and gave me a renewed energy to do so.

Jesus often took time to pause. In the midst of His busiest schedule, at times of great stress and pressure, He stepped away from the realities of His physical life and communicated with His Father. The results are evident in the Gospels. He met with His Father and calmed the waters. He met with His Father and healed the sick. He met with His father and cast out demons. He met with His Father and went to the cross.

A time away to focus on God gives new strength, new power, new energy for the tasks God asks us to do. The prophet Isaiah said - "... those who hope in the Lord will renew their strength" (Is.40:31). We are all living on the edge of life, the edge of death. Perhaps it's time to gain a little perspective and renew our energy. Perhaps we should all make it a daily habit.

****

Buried Beacons and God's Eye

"E.T.A., Fourteen hundred hours." Chuck had been waiting to hear the message come crackling over the radio. "Roger that, I'll be ready. Mallack Dome clear." His shift as radio operator at the temporary airstrip was over and he was anxious to leave his isolated northern post. The plane was on its way and would arrive in just over three hours. Chuck immediately set to work packing up his belongings and the equipment he had used to do his job. The site was to be abandoned for the time being, so everything had to be packed securely and made ready to go.

When he was done, Chuck sat by the radio again, waiting for the pilot to let him know when he was on approach. It seemed like a long wait. Then he heard the unmistakable sound of an engine. Surprised that the pilot had not radioed, he went outside to check. Sure enough, off in the distance was a small speck making a lot of noise. He went back in and sat by the radio. Still no message from the pilot. The sound of the plane seemed to be fading away. Chuck ran outside just in time to see the speck disappear. At the sound of radio static, he dashed back in to hear, "Mallack Dome, come in. Mallack Dome, are you awake down there?" Chuck grabbed the microphone and answered. The pilot responded immediately. "Check your beacon, Chuck. I can't find you."

Chuck's jaw fell open. In his urgency to get everything ready, he had disconnected and packed the electronic signal beacon. In the vast Arctic tundra, it was impossible for the pilot to locate him without it. "Uh, roger that. Checking beacon. Stand by one." In a panic, Chuck found and reinstalled the beacon and heaved a sigh of relief as the sound of the plane's engine got louder and louder.

Many of us have buried our signal beacons. Whether intentionally, because we have been rejected and hurt, or because we have been preoccupied and selfish, we have hidden the things that send clear messages to those around us. As a result, they have no idea how we really feel or what we really think. They aren't able to find us.

Many of us attempt to do this with God. We bury

our true feelings and thoughts, refusing to acknowledge them even to ourselves. We try to hide them from God. We think we will escape His eye. But God doesn't need a beacon. He is aware of where we are, how we are, why we are, at all times. Psalm 139:1-3 says, "O Lord, you have searched me and you know me. You know when I sit and when I rise; you perceive my thoughts from afar. You discern my going out and my lying down; you are familiar with all my ways."

Does that make you uncomfortable? Too much like 'Big Brother is watching?' Not to worry. God's motives are pure. His eye is on us, not waiting to humiliate and destroy, but to guide, nurture and bless. The writer of this Psalm acknowledges there is nowhere he can hide where God will not find him. And what happens when He does? Listen to verse 10 - "even there your hand will guide me, your right hand will hold me fast."

****

Finding Your Way Home

I was on a plane somewhere over the Atlantic Ocean when I had the first dream. As most dreams are, it was confusing, full of images and scraps of sound that, though vivid and realistic were disjointed and without logical sequence. I had another similar dream on the bus taking me to my hometown back in Canada, then another on the train north, taking me to the isolated fishing lodge where I was to work for the summer. The dreams were full of foreign scenes – orange-tiled roofs and dark-skinned children from Spain, cheese shops and narrow streets from France, soaring mountains and towering cathedrals from Switzerland.

The trip from Lisbon to my destination in northern Ontario took about 36 hours. By the time I arrived I was disoriented, but had no time to think about it. I went to work immediately and didn't have a chance to relax until later that day when I went for a swim. Floating on a small raft, I soon was dozing in the warm sun. Again, dreams filled my mind with disorienting images and sounds. Then my foot slipped off the raft into the icy water. I woke with a start, staring at a landscape that shocked me. There were no red-tiled roofs or foreign languages, no Gothic cathedrals or cobblestone streets. My eyes opened to rugged cliffs and swaying pines. I knew I was not in Spain, but where was I? Then I realized, "Oh. Canada.

I'm home." Home - the place where I was safe, where everything was familiar – the landscape, the culture, the language.

We all need that place called home. We need to know we are safe and surrounded by what is familiar. But sometimes we can feel as though we are living in a foreign land, surrounded by strangers speaking words we can't understand. Sometimes we feel so out of place that every day is a struggle, a battle to believe we belong. The battle is real because the truth is we don't belong. We weren't made to live in this world of corruption and chaos. We were made to live in a climate of joy and praise, in the presence of God. Anything less will make us feel disjointed, out of place. Anything less will leave us with a longing for home.

Our home is not a place, not a city nor a country field, not a valley nor a mountaintop. Our home is with God. "Therefore, since we have been justified through faith, we have peace with God through our Lord Jesus Christ through whom we have gained access by faith into this grace in which we now stand. And we rejoice in the hope of the glory of God" (Romans 5:1, 2). Peace with God brings us home, no matter where we are, no matter what our circumstances. Jesus brings us home.

****

Miracles in the Skies

Many of us try to avoid the television coverage of the anniversary of 9/11. For some it's a matter of resisting the media hype. For others, the pain depicted is just too much to watch, yet again. But the media coverage is hard to avoid. It caught up with me late one night as I found myself watching a CBC documentary about Canadian reporters who covered the tragedy and Canadian politicians who were forced to deal with various aspects of it. It was a perspective I found intriguing and one which revealed a whole new aspect of that horrible day. It also revealed one of the miracles.

Being the wife of a one-time air traffic controller, I was particularly struck by interviews with those involved in shutting down the skies across our country. Their decision to divert air traffic to remote areas on the coast was covered in the press at the time, along with stories about the tremendous hospitality shown by small communities where the planes landed. But the magnitude of what that process involved did not occur to me until I watched the anniversary coverage.

I was amazed at one visual image of a map of Canada and the U.S., so criss-crossed by flight paths that it glowed brighter than any Christmas tree ever could. Tiny blips, representing huge airliners, were shown circling, descending, veering in every direction, as controllers guided them down to safe landing strips across the country. As I watched the patterns slowly dissolve on their screens, I suddenly realized I was watching the visual depiction of a modern-day miracle. Not one of those planes crashed. None collided in midair. No accidents, neither through the fault of man nor machine, occurred. Considering the volume of air traffic across this continent that was a miracle.

That miracle happened in the skies above us on Sept. 11, 2001, but most of us were too focused on the attack and the drama unfolding on the ground to be concerned with what was happening in the air. But there was a crew of committed men and women who did their jobs, preserving thousands of lives in the process. You might say they were the unsung angels of 9/11.

Some day, perhaps, we will stand in awe of what has gone on in the spiritual realm while we had our eyes focused on the ground. Like Elisha's servant, we will see the host of heaven around us and be amazed. "Then the Lord opened the servant's eyes and he looked and saw the hills full of horses and chariots of fire all around Elisha" (2 Kings 6:17). It will happen, some day, but even now, if you watch closely, you can see the miracles unfold. Sometimes they're right there on T.V.

A Mountain Experience

It is said, in ancient times the Japanese worshiped Mt. Fuji. Mt. Kilimanjaro in Africa was also revered in times gone by. I thought it absurd that rational people would do such a thing, until an experience in Alaska opened my mind. I was flying from Anchorage to Fairbanks. It was a beautiful day, the plane flying high above a ridge of mountains forming an arch across the land. The tips of the peaks were far below, looking like a row of up-turned pointed paper cups. Pretty, but not terribly impressive. I watched the shadow of our plane slide over them and was musing on the amazing ingenuity and intelligence of man when the shadow began to shift.

Slowly it moved up, as though sliding on a string. My eyes followed it until it was swallowed by cloud. When the plane broke through my mind ran full force into something so overwhelming it literally took my breath away. There before us stood Mt. McKinley, its glaciers gleaming in the sun, its base obscured by cloud, its peak rising so high above us I had to slump in my seat to see it. Our plane was now a tiny sliver of tin edging its way by. The word awesome does not do it justice.

Perhaps I was all the more amazed because I had lived at the base of that mountain for two months. It became so familiar I hardly took notice of it. I did not realize I had only seen its base, the part below the mist and cloud. As I stared, I knew why people would worship a mountain.

I also had a new understanding of how we fail to see the God who created us. We live at the base of the mountain and most of its beauty is almost always obscured. We cannot see all of God in His majesty and glory. Moses asked for that privilege and God was gracious. He told Moses to stand on a rock, then said, "When my glory passes by, I will put you in a cleft in the rock and cover you with my hand until I have passed by. Then I will remove my hand and you will see my back; but my face must not be seen" (Exodus 33:22&23). Many wonder why God is so diligent about keeping Himself hidden. As I remember Mt. McKinley I wonder if it may be in part so we do not grow too familiar with Him. Would we take him for granted as I did Mt. McKinley? It's hard to believe that's possible, yet we already do. We take for granted the amazing complexity of the world around us, the beauty laid out for us each day, the "small" miracles of life and death, like the "small" mountains I found so unimpressive. Perhaps as we learn to appreciate these, the cloud thins a little. God reveals Himself in it all.

Psalm 19:1&2 says, "The heavens declare the glory of God; the skies proclaim the work of His hands. Day after day they pour forth speech; night after night they display knowledge." The Psalm goes on to describe the goodness of God's Word. The scriptures, like the world around us, paint a portrait of God. He has revealed Himself. Perhaps much of the obscuring cloud is of our own making. Perhaps He's just waiting for us to look up and see.

****

The Jungle Canopy and the Hand of God

The tropical sun was just beginning to rise as we shouldered our packs and headed off. The trek would take about five hours, maybe less if the trail was dry. I had been praying ever since we set the date for this visit in the Sepik Province of Papua New Guinea. I had seen pictures of what that trail through the rain forest was like when it was wet. I knew the intensity of the tropical sun. I knew if it took most people five hours, it might take me eight. We crossed the river just as the sun's glare rose above the horizon. I heard one of the men comment in Pidgin English that the level was low. I thanked God. We followed the riverbank for a while, then struck off into the jungle, leaving all sign of the village behind.

As I entered the rainforest, I felt the awe and tinge of fear at being in a foreign place, a place so far removed from my normal environment that it left my senses tingling. Insects buzzed and hummed and whined incessantly. The thick jungle shivered and sighed as unseen creatures moved about around us. Now and then we heard the unmistakable raucous noise of a hornbill's wings (a friend describes it as a helicopter with asthma), and the clap of the egrets and whoosh of cockatoos high above. We chatted as we walked, sipped often from our water bottles, and stopped to rest at each river fording. As I waded across the shallow water of the second crossing, I realized I was thoroughly enjoying myself.

Almost five hours later, I realized I was exhausted. With great relief I heard the throb of the plane's engine as it made its descent onto the grass airstrip. A few minutes later we stepped out onto the open field. I staggered at the heat. It was not until then I realized how much we had been protected from the full force of the sun by the thick canopy of green above us. I knew I would not have been able to make it to the airstrip if we had been walking in the open. Without the protection of the canopy, the sun would have beaten us all.

God's protection is just as vital. As the canopy in a rainforest shelters what is below, God shelters His people. As we would be beaten down and overcome by the severity of the tropical sun, we would be unable to survive without the covering protection of our God.

Isaiah 51:16 says, "I have...covered you with the shadow of my hand - I who set the heavens in place, who laid the foundations of the earth..."

Are you aware of His protection? Do you realize that without it you would cease to exist? Acknowledge the One who shelters you in the shadow of His hand. Thank Him. Adore Him. Then bask in the shade of His canopy.

****

The Seeds of Discovery

My husband and I watched a film recently that had a lot to do with discovery. A man with a brilliant brain, insatiable curiosity and more than a little ambition set himself and others on a path that led to the development of aviation. Their achievements were astounding. It seemed their motto was, "The sky is no limit." We have comfortable air travel and satellite T.V. today because they believed it.

I couldn't help but wonder what made the minds of those men work the way they did. What would make a man think of flying in the first place? What would make a man think that by putting an orbiting satellite into space we could have instant pictures on a screen in our living rooms?

I asked myself a similar question one day in the jungles of Papua New Guinea. I was with a group of women who had gone deep into the Sago swamps to harvest their main source of food. The first step was to chop down a Sago palm. Then the women lined up along its length and began hacking at it until the entire trunk was reduced to a pile of sawdust. The shavings were carried to the river where another group had prepared a long trough made out of another tree. The shavings were piled into the hollow of the trunk and then water was poured over them. The water leached the starch from the shavings and was collected in a large pot. When it was boiled the starch formed a gelatinous lump that was then formed into a dumpling or dried like a pancake. As I watched, I wondered how on earth these people had discovered that such a laborious process would yield an edible result?

There is a verse in the Bible that gives us a clue. The Apostle James wrote, "Every good and perfect gift is from above, coming down from the Father of the heavenly lights, who does not change like shifting shadows" (James 1:17). The discoveries made by man that have enriched our lives are certainly good and perfect, because they were designed for us, not by brilliant men, but by our creator.

The seeds of discovery are planted by God. He is the primary engineer, the first gardener, the creator of it all. The discoveries of flight are miniscule when you place them beside the creation of the heavens. The discoveries of agriculture are infinitesimal when you place them beside the creation of the earth itself.

The Apostle Paul said it in another way – "For every house is built by someone but God is the builder of everything" (Hebrews 3:4).

The inventors of aviation and every other field are honored as heroes. How then should we respond to God? Should we not praise? Should we not be thankful?

****

Too Much Baggage

The airport was huge. Walking in step with the crowd that had just deplaned, I felt somewhat like a sheep in the midst of the herd, hoping we were going the right way. As I watched for signs to the baggage carousels, I began to wish I hadn't brought such a large and heavy carry-on bag. My pace began to slow and soon I was at the tail end of the crowd. It was then I noticed the heads of some of the people, gliding by without the usual bob of those who were walking. As the crowd thinned, I saw that those people were not walking, but standing on a conveyor belt, their bags at their feet. It was some time before I was able to step up onto it and put my suitcase at my feet. It was a relief to lay it down.

I watched the rest of the crowd striding by, most of them carrying bags of one sort or another, some of them struggling to do so. I wondered why they didn't hop on the conveyor. They could see it, they could see those who were gliding by without effort, yet they continued to struggle. I wondered if it was just a matter of pride, a decision to do it without help, perhaps a fear that others might think them lazy. Then I realized there was one advantage to walking. The conveyor was slow. Those who walked, even with heavy bags, were able to move a bit faster in their dash for the exits. But in the end we all ended up at the same place, waiting for the rest of our baggage to arrive. Those who had walked just had a bit longer to stand and wait.

I thought of the scripture in which Jesus asks us to lean on Him, to depend on Him for support. He says, "Come to me, all you who are weary and burdened and I will give you rest. Take my yoke upon you and learn from me, for I am gentle and humble in heart, and you will find rest for your souls. For my yoke is easy and my burden is light" (Matthew 11:28-30).

Many of us refuse God's offer because we are too proud. Some of us don't want to be seen as weak, in need of help. Some of us are too impatient, not willing to stay within God's timetable. In the end, however, we will all arrive at the same place, standing before Him. Like those arriving at the baggage carousels in an airport, we will all be waiting to see what comes next. For those who have leaned on God, those who have taken the time to get to know Him, there will be the reward of eternal life with Him.

Are you struggling through life without help? Jesus wants to share your burdens. Isn't it time you put them down at His feet?

****

Two Days After

The line of people snaked through Toronto's Pearson Airport with a low hum of conversation, broken now and then by the buzz of electronic devices - hair dryers and razors being plugged in, to prove they weren't fake. Armed men roamed through the crowd. At the counter, luggage was opened, personal belongings tossed about, nail files and fingernail clippers taken out, purses and briefcases tagged. One woman looked embarrassed at needing a stranger's help to get her suitcase closed again. Another looked flustered as a long screwdriver was pulled from her handbag. "I forgot it was in there," she explained. The security guard wasn't smiling. One man said, "They can search me six ways to Sunday. The more they do, the more secure I feel." It was two days after 9/11.

As I waited in the departure lounge hours later, I realized not many people looked like they felt secure. Most were fidgeting, some pacing. All were taking careful note of those who would be boarding the same plane. A tall man standing by the window seemed especially diligent. He was not looking out the window, but studying the people. I noticed him survey each person's bag, his eyes lingering on each purse, each briefcase. He also studied the faces, his eyes not shifting away when they looked directly at him. As we boarded the plane, he stood behind the stewardess, watching.

Security. It is a word we hear continually, in the aftermath of the attack on the World Trade Center on September 11, 2001. No doubt many will continually wonder, how secure are we, really? Will the security measures taken at airports and borders really make a difference? Will all the efforts to protect the western world from another such attack guarantee it won't happen again? The underlying reality creeps from beneath these questions - there is no guarantee. Must we then, like the people of so many other countries, live in constant fear? Must we change our daily habits and train our children to do likewise? No doubt our lives have changed as a result of the attack on the United States, but there is one constant that remains.

Psalm 112:6-8 says, "Surely he will never be shaken; a righteous man will be remembered forever. He will have no fear of bad news; his heart is steadfast, trusting in the Lord. His heart is secure, he will have no fear." The only real security lies in trusting God. Putting your faith in Jesus guarantees, not a life without conflict or stress, but a life of peace in spite of circumstances, a calm heart that conquers fear.

"So we say with confidence, "The Lord is my helper; I will not be afraid. What can man do to me?"" (Hebrews 13:6).

Boarding a 757 two days after one was used as a flying bomb did make me realize Jesus is the only guarantee.

****

2 ON THE ROAD

Aren't We There Yet?

I remember the back seat of my dad's car. If I close my eyes I can see it, smell it, feel it. When I was a child I spent a lot of time there. We lived on an island fifty miles from town. All our relatives lived more than 500 miles away. The frequent long drives seemed interminable and I know my parents got tired of hearing me say those familiar words - "Are we there yet?"

When the Bible was written, almost 2,000 years ago, the people were anticipating an arrival. They were looking for the promised Messiah. Those who believed in Jesus and followed His teaching knew the Messiah had arrived. They thought He was going to stay around for a while, build His kingdom and free them from the tyranny of the Romans. They did not anticipate His early departure, but they were greatly encouraged by His promise to return, and "soon."

To those who read the Bible now, that promise begs the answer to one question: "Why hasn't He come back? It's been 2,000 years. Aren't we there yet?!"

The answer can be given in terms of kids on a long voyage. Their perspective is that the trip is taking forever. Each minute seems like an hour. They don't want to sit back and enjoy the drive. They don't use the time constructively. They don't pay much attention to the milestones they pass along the way. They just want to be there.

Imagine a pilot in an airplane high above them. His perspective is complete. He sees where they began and where they are going. He knows what's going on at that moment all along the road, and he knows how long it will take them to get there. He knows it's a journey they must take and there are important things for them to do along the way. He can see that their journey is only a short distance compared to the length of the whole road.

God's perspective is like that pilot. He stands beyond time and knows the journey we are on. It will take no less and no more time than necessary. There are milestones to notice along the way, much to do and much to enjoy as we go.

Matthew 24 and 25 talk about the return of Jesus and much is said about the journey. We are told to be occupied with the work God has given us to do, to be faithful. Above all, we are told to "keep watch," to continue to anticipate His arrival. To those who do, Jesus will say, as in Matthew 25: 23, "Well done, good and faithful servant!....come and share your master's happiness!"

Jesus will return some day, and at just the right time. No, we're not there yet, but we're getting there!

****

A Long Lonely Road

I once made a discovery. There are not many people on the highways of northern Saskatchewan on a Sunday morning. My husband and I had attended a conference there and unfortunately he took ill on Saturday night, so rather than attend the church service as planned, we decided to run for home. His illness had high-jacked our plans. We left as soon as we were able Sunday morning.

I don't usually like driving for that length of time; I have a hard time staying awake after three to four hours. I knew my husband would sleep most of the way, and I can't drink regular coffee, so I started praying that the Lord would keep me alert. I knew there would not be much to look at as we drove. Or so I thought.

Early spring is a rather melancholy time to drive the prairies. Everything is a pale tawny brown – no shoots of life showing yet. We saw a small group of pronghorn antelope – just in time to slow down and avoid hitting one of them. They were the color of the prairie but for their distinctive white markings. The skies were the color of lead and a faint haze often sprayed the windshield. The last of the snow had melted that week, leaving large pools of water on the surface of the ground. Birds were everywhere. We saw flocks of Canada geese, hundreds of ducks and large graceful white swans flying high on their way north.

As our vehicle sped across the prairie I thought of how tiny we would seem to those birds looking down from such a height. Compared to their fragility, I tended to think of us as the stronger entity, but then I thought of how they would see us. Our vehicle probably looked like a dinky toy, its noise muffled or perhaps even muted by the distance. To those birds, we were probably quite insignificant as they set about their purpose in migration. We weren't even a small distraction to them.

Then I pondered how God sees us from on high. We aren't a distraction to Him, either. We are His focus. How astounding to realize that! God's eyes are continually on each of us, whether we are sitting in our living room, in a church sanctuary, or speeding across a lonely prairie at 100 kilometers an hour. He knows where we are, He's watching out for us, and He cares where we are going.

King David's Psalm 121 states this plainly. He tells the people of Israel, "… the Lord will watch over your coming and going both now and forevermore" (Psalm 121:8).

The Lord did keep me awake and alert on that lonely drive across the prairie. He gave me lots to see and lots to think about. Wherever we are, He is there - above us, before us, behind us and beside us. With us always. What a comfort!

****

A Mini Parked Between Semis

I gripped the wheel of my Austin Mini and concentrated on the flow of traffic around me. I had never driven through this area before but I knew the route I had to follow would take me through the heart of a large city. There was no bypass to avoid the downtown traffic. I stayed in the middle lane to avoid vehicles turning left and right. As the city began to close around me, so did the traffic. I was already feeling a bit claustrophobic when a huge semi pulled up to my right. We both stopped at a red light.

Then another semi pulled up on my left. The two trucks effectively blocked out the sun. I glanced in my rear-view mirror just as a third semi pulled in behind me, stopping inches from my tiny bumper. Suddenly I realized my palms were sweaty. I concentrated on the stoplight and the instant it changed to green, my little car sped forward, out from under those looming shadows. I'm sure those truck drivers had a good laugh at my expense. I don't know if they had intended to intimidate me, but they certainly succeeded in doing so.

I thought of that incident some time ago while talking with a woman whose life was in turmoil. A few months ago her life had been broadsided when her husband was struck with a serious illness. She was just coming to terms with that when she herself was hospitalized. She was still trying to catch her breath when a third tragedy struck. As she described what had happened, she shook her head and made a revealing statement. "Somehow in the middle of it all, I managed to hang on to one thought. God would get me through it. As long as I focused on Him I was okay, but the minute I focused on what was happening around me, I could feel the panic rising."

I remembered looking in the rear-view mirror of my Austin Mini and seeing nothing but bumper. I remembered how those semis had blocked out the sun. And I remembered focusing on that stop-light, knowing that it would eventually turn green and let me get out of there. Sometimes life puts us in a box of pain and confusion. The only way to survive is to hang on to the One you know will get you out.

Are you feeling trapped in a dark place? Focusing on the character of God will lift you beyond circumstances, giving peace and assurance. Know He is good; know He will never abandon you; know He loves you unconditionally. Know the light will eventually turn green. Say, with the Psalmist David, "But as for me, I will always have hope; I will praise you more and more. My mouth will tell of your righteousness, of your salvation all day long, though I know not its measure.... you will restore my life again" (Psalm 71:14-20).

****

A Wrong Turn to The Right Place

The morning dawned bright with the promise of another blistering hot day. My husband was glad he had gotten up at 5:30 a.m. to begin our trip home after a pleasant stay in one of Idaho's State parks. Most of the driving would be done in the cooler morning hours and he wouldn't have to listen to the moans and groans about not having an air-conditioned R.V. On the outskirts of Spokane, he spotted the sign directing traffic onto Hwy 22 North, and maneuvered our unit easily along the freeway, hours before the congestion of the city's rush hour.

Things were going just fine until he saw a sign stating the mileage to the Washington/Idaho border. He thought that was a bit odd since he had just left Idaho, but carried on. A few more pleasant miles down the road he saw another sign saying, Sand Point, 15 miles. Now he knew there was something amiss. Sand Point was in Idaho, only a few miles from where we had started at 5:30 that morning. He pulled over to consult the map. I heard the groan from my comfort zone in the back.

Highway 22 was the right road, but we were headed in the wrong direction. Highway 22 North took us in a complete circle back to where we had started. A few miles further into Spokane there was a second exit for Highway 22 West, which would put us on the road back to Canada. More groans. Oh well, at least we were parked in front of a restaurant. Breakfast brightened the mood somewhat until we returned to the camper, which was already heating up like an oven. Repeated attempts to get the key to start the engine resulted in silence. Well, silence from the engine, that is.

As my husband checked under the hood, I prayed this would be something simple and cheap to fix. We had to wait two hours before any of the local garages opened up. The mechanic was as mystified as Spence. For some reason the battery was completely dead, but the alternator had been replaced only a couple of days before and seemed to be working well. A couple of hours later a complete check of the system revealed a plug hanging loose. It was jammed in between the wiring and had appeared to be connected but was not. The motor home had been running on the battery and eventually it ran out. Well, it was a simple problem to fix and it was cheap. A little embarrassing, but cheap. In a short time we headed off again, back to Spokane (during rush hour), and Highway 22 West.

It wasn't until we were out into the rolling, dry country of northern Washington that we realized how God had taken care of us. There were no towns, no cool restaurants, no garages with friendly mechanics on that road. It was miles and miles of open wheat lands, beautiful to watch as we rolled by in the almost-comfort of our hot R.V., but undoubtedly miserable to stare at from a hot R.V. broken down on a narrow shoulder. If we had been on this road when we wanted to be, it would have been an unpleasant and costly experience indeed.

Sometimes our lives take wrong turns. Due to circumstances beyond our control, we end up going in a direction we haven't chosen. Knowing God has a plan makes a big difference in how we respond. And He does have a plan, as Proverbs 19:21 tells us – "Many are the plans in a man's heart, but it is the Lord's purpose that prevails." Do you know God's purpose for your life? Does it seem like you're on the wrong road going in the wrong direction? Discover His plan for you and the journey will be joyful.

****

A Condition that Got Results

   It was a beautiful fall day and I was looking forward to the trip to town. We pulled out of our driveway onto the road that connected to the highway, bordering our land. I peered down the long stretch and sighed. As my husband maneuvered the truck slowly down the road, I clutched his arm and held onto my stomach. By the time we reached the highway, Spence had a few finger-sized bruises and I had a few more stretch marks. You see, I was eight months pregnant and the road was full of potholes big enough to swallow a cow (no comparison intended).

   The territorial road crew was supposed to grade that road. It had been part of the original route between Whitehorse and Dawson City at one time, so, when we built our house, the government assured us they would maintain it. That summer had been wet and the crews had spent most of their time on the roads leading to the gold mines. Our road was not a priority. Several times my husband had politely requested they do some work on it, to no avail. That day I decided it was time I paid the road crew foreman a visit.

Charlie was a big gruff man, but he had a heart of gold. When he saw me lumber into his office, he stood up quickly and offered me a chair. I immediately stated the obvious. "Charlie, I'm pregnant," I said. "I'm looking forward to having this baby, but I do not want to have it on the road between my house and the highway!" Charlie's eyes bulged. His face went a bit red and he started to stammer. He assured me he would take care of it right away. By the time we arrived home, the road had been surfaced and graded. It was in better shape than the main highway! My husband was astounded and suggested that, after the baby was born, I should get one of those pregnancy simulating forms, to put on whenever we needed something done. I wasn't sure that was such a great idea, but I could see his point. My condition had definitely gotten the results we wanted. All I had to do was bring it to the attention of the right person.

Sometimes we wonder if God notices our condition. We go through pain and grief and hard times and we wonder if He knows. We see the wrongs done and we tend to say, "Hey, God, did you see that?!" Sometimes we forget who we're talking to. God is not a maintenance man who has to be shown the urgency of our situation. He is the One who sees and knows all things. Psalm 139:1-3 says, "O Lord ... You know when I sit down or stand up. You know my every thought ... Every moment you know where I am."

He knows. He sees. He is responding. Trust Him.

****

From White Knuckles to Praise

It was a dark and stormy day. The clouds were low and unloading a torrent of rain as I drove home from the city. It wasn't quite time to be driving with headlights on, but all the vehicles around me were because of the poor visibility. I drove with both hands on the wheel and was soon feeling the tension in my back and neck. It was going to be a long ride home so I decided I needed a little company. I picked out a CD I purchased at a conference a few months ago and popped it into the player. The singer, Ali Matthews, was part of the entertainment one night and she had impressed me with the clarity of her voice and the lyrics of her songs.

It wasn't long before I was singing along with her – singing songs of praise, songs about God's amazing care for us. It wasn't long before my car felt like a comfortable cocoon. I was warm, dry and safe inside as I sensed God's presence with me, right there in the middle of that dark and stormy day as trucks whooshed by in sprays of water, obliterating my view of the road. As I pulled onto the exit ramp into my home town about an hour later, I realized what a difference that music had made. My grip on the steering wheel had relaxed; my neck and back were no longer stiff. And my mind was not focused on the storm, but on the glory of a loving God who is with us all, no matter our circumstances.

The Prophet Isaiah recorded God's promise to us – "Fear not. For I have redeemed you; I have called you by name; you are mine. When you pass through the waters, I will be with you; and when you pass through the rivers, they will not sweep over you. When you walk through the fire, you will not be burned; the flames will not set you ablaze. For I am the Lord, your God, the Holy One of Israel, your Savior" (Isaiah 43:1-3).

Even on a dark and stormy day - or night - we can know that God is with us, that He will take us through any circumstance this world can throw at us. All we have to do is remember to focus on Him, lean on Him, cry out to Him. He's always there, just waiting to respond.

****

Doubts in the Storm

Signs of winter were everywhere: clouds getting lower and more gray, the sun rising later and falling sooner, the Yukon river icing on its edges. The indicators put pressure on Monna, who needed to make a trip into Alaska over the Top of the World Highway. The date was past the cut-off date, when the road was deemed too dangerous to drive, so we discussed alternatives, but she was determined to make the trip and she wanted me to go with her. She assured me the highway crew would keep the road clear for miners still up there. Against my better judgment, I found myself in the passenger seat the next morning, as we crossed the Yukon river and headed for Alaska.

The first part of the trip was pleasant. We chatted, enjoying the view as the road climbed. Wind rocked the vehicle as trees became scarce and snow fell. The higher we went, the thicker the snow. Eventually we were plowing through it. Three times we dug through wind-hardened drifts. We considered turning around, but by then it was too late - forward or back, we were in the middle of a blizzard. "But the grader will be along soon," Monna said, "and I'm praying."

Not being a believer then, I doubted prayer would

help, but did believe the grader would clear the road. Then, two miles from the border, we hit a drift too deep and wide to dig through. Sitting in the car, the heater roaring, we watched the snow bury us. Every few minutes we'd shovel the car clear to make sure the grader operator could see us in the swirling white. As the minutes ticked past the first hour and the gas gauge slipped below the half way mark, I mentally went through the survival gear we had brought.

And I wondered if the grader operator would keep going in this weather. As the time ticked into the second hour my fears spilled out. "What if the grader broke down? What if he took the day off?"

Monna peered into the storm and wondered about walking to the border. As the gas gauge slipped below the final quarter mark and the light began to fade, we knew we might have no other choice. "The grader will come," Monna said.

I kept my doubts to myself. In the middle of the tense silence Monna turned off the ignition. All we heard was the roar of wind. Then another sound penetrated, a mechanical sound. We leaped out in time to see pulsing beams of light round the bend, cutting through the snow. We waved our arms as the grader maneuvered around the car. "Salvation" had come.

Doubt isn't bad. It can lead to faith. Confusion leads

to questions, which can lead to clarity. Fear causes us to seek solutions beyond ourselves and that can lead to God. The key is to not allow doubt, fear and confusion to overwhelm and paralyze. The key is to look for our salvation in the right place.

When Jesus was crucified, His followers doubted. How could the kingdom be established when the king was dead? Had He lied to them? Then Jesus stepped into their midst. At first they doubted their own eyes, and probably their sanity as well, until He spoke and "opened their minds so they could understand..." (Luke 24:45). His appearance brought clarity, peace and faith to His followers then, and He will bring it to us now, if we turn our hearts to Him. Isaiah 30:15 says, "In repentance and rest is your salvation, in quietness and trust is your strength..."

In the midst of a storm, doubt, fear and confusion are natural. In the midst of a storm, faith, peace and clarity are possible. Repent, rest, trust, and listen for the Savior's voice.

****

Frightening Facts and A Note of Hope

Driving long distances alone has never been my favorite thing to do, but sometimes it has its benefits. I can sit alone with my own thoughts, giving me time to sort out things that have been on my mind. Short stories have been virtually written on long drives. Essays and speeches have been fine-tuned. Sometimes it's nice to just turn the dial on the radio and find something worth listening to. As I drove to Calgary some time ago I decided to see what the airwaves had to offer.

CBC caught my attention. The man being interviewed had a long list of credentials. He was a scientist, a specialist in entomology, climatology and the environment. I was fascinated by what he had to say. It seems he and several of his colleagues have been compiling statistics on the frequency and ferocity of natural disasters over the last two decades; they have studied the resulting effects on natural habitats. What they discovered has alarmed them.

It seems the weather patterns across the globe are showing signs of being erratic and out of control. The resulting droughts, floods and earthquakes have wrecked havoc, not only in material loss and human death, but in terms of the disruption of the natural patterns of animals and insects. This in turn is beginning to result in significant spread of disease. A virus carried by the large bats of Southeast Asia, for instance, was transferred into pigs and then into humans when the bats were displaced by prolonged drought. Hundreds of people died and the World

Health Organization now fears this virus may spread.

As I listened to this man, his voice at times took on a decidedly urgent tone. He's worried. And he's not the only one. We keep hearing rumors of disasters of global proportions. We keep seeing the devastation across the globe from natural disasters and shifting weather patterns. The television reports on wars and famines daily. And we're worried too.

Many Christians point at all of these things and then to their Bibles. There is a great deal of catastrophe prophesied in the scriptures. The Apostle Matthew warned about it when he said, "You will hear of wars and rumors of wars, but see to it that you are not alarmed" (Matthew 24:6).

And we might respond, "Easy for you to say!" How do we remain at peace in times such as these? The answer lies in many other scriptures that talk about God's sovereignty. He is in control. Matthew himself says, "these things must happen." He knows God is unfolding His plan. We can know it too. He will never relinquish His sovereignty over our world. We can say with the writer of the most prophetic book in the Bible, "our Lord God Almighty reigns" (Rev. 19:6b).

That scientist had all the statistics and data at his fingertips. The facts told him to expect trouble. We have the Word of God at our fingertips. It tells us to watch, be vigilant, pray and trust God.

****

Are You Good to Go?

"Are you good to go?" My daughter stood at the door, pulling her jacket on as she reached for the doorknob. She was impatient to be on her way.

The day before I'd been at a funeral. A good friend was facing major surgery, and I'd just received an email asking for prayer for a man with an inoperable brain tumor. So my daughter's expression struck me differently than it might have, under other circumstances. It's the lot of a minister's wife to be often faced with thoughts of death. When your life's work deals with God, it deals with what comes after. When death looms, people seek spiritual counsel and encouragement. When they are staring into eternity, they start wondering about God and what really happens when the heart stops beating.

Death can seem to be a morbid subject. For many, it's a subject they studiously avoid. People hate change and death is the ultimate change. Whether you believe in an afterlife or not, death's reality forces a change that cannot be controlled, cannot be scheduled, cannot be evaded. Best not to think about it. Avoid hospitals.

Ignore the statistics about cancer and heart disease.
Avoid churches. Avoid God. Put the blinders on and
just keep going. Until someone asks a question, like,
"Are you good to go?" Or how about this one – "If
you die today, where will you spend eternity?"

Jesus has freed us from the fear of death. The
apostle Paul recognized this when he stated, "For to
me, to live is Christ and to die is gain." He lived his life
knowing God was dwelling in him. Therefore, he had
no fear of death. He knew that whatever death might
bring, whatever it looked like, it would be a reunion
with Christ. We, too, can know where we are going.
We can be "good to go" at any given moment. John
3:14 says, "Just as Moses lifted up the snake in the
desert, so the Son of Man must be lifted up, that
everyone who believes in Him may have eternal life."
It takes just a simple step, a simple sentence,
whispered from the heart, an invitation for God to be
part of your life now, and forever.

I love Romans 14:8 – "If we live, we live to the
Lord; and if we die, we die to the Lord. So, whether
we live or die, we belong to the Lord." Death holds no
fear, for those who believe that sentence.

All of us are standing at the doorway to eternity. You
may not realize you have your jacket on and your hand
on the doorknob. Are you "good to go?"

****

Ice Flows and other Dangerous Traps

Chuck's truck idled gently as he and his wife peered through the windshield at the view of Hunker Creek Road. They watched the slow seepage from a small glacier flow over the ploughed surface and they hesitated. They knew what it would mean if they got stuck trying to cross that patch of ice. The small glaciers are a common winter hazard in that area. The seepage can look like a trickle but the constant flow and freeze wrecks havoc on anything in its path. Like the huge glaciers we study about in school, the movement of these small ice fields is unstoppable.

But Chuck decided no trickle of water and ice was going to stop him. He put the truck into gear and moved forward. They were about half way across the patch of ice and water when the tires started to spin. Chuck lifted his foot off the accelerator, then slowly applied pressure again. The tires spun and the rear end slipped. He tried again and the truck slid sideways. One rear wheel was now off the road entirely. For the next few hours Chuck and his wife tried everything they could think of to get that truck out of that dangerous place, but their attempts were futile. As night began to fall they realize they would have to leave the truck there and try again the next day. By the time they returned, their vehicle was completely off the road and solidly locked in ice.

By the spring thaw, they found it part way down the hill. It was mid summer before the ice had thawed enough to attempt the salvage. Chuck hoped the Caterpillar tractor he hired to pull it out wouldn't bend the frame any more than the glacier already had. Vehicles had been known to be bent beyond use by similar slow "trickles of water and ice."

We have those same inexorable trickles in our lives. They are small things we think we can live with, things we don't want to acknowledge as having any power over us. These small things have a way of creeping up on us, like that glacier Chuck thought he could handle. It doesn't take long before we're stuck. The writer of James 1:14-16 says, "But each one is dragged away and enticed. Then, after desire has conceived it gives birth to sin and sin, when it is full-grown, gives birth to death. Don't be deceived …"

Chuck thought he could beat the glacier. He lost. Don't think you can live with sin and win. There's only one way to stop it, as James goes on to say in verse 21, "So get rid of all the filth and evil in your lives and humbly accept the message God has planted in your hearts, for it its strong enough to save your souls."

****

Just Follow Me

We were in a strange city whose streets seemed to have no logical pattern and whose drivers seemed to like excessive speed. I wasn't happy about having to drive through the heart of it. "Don't worry," my husband said. "Just stay close and follow me."

He jumped into our newly purchased vehicle and zipped into the flow of traffic. I gripped the steering wheel and followed. At the second intersection he zoomed through a yellow light that turned red before I could advance. The instant it turned green I sped forward, trying to peer over and around the cars ahead, hoping to catch sight of my husband and our new car. I didn't know that when he was several blocks ahead he realized I was no longer behind him, so he pulled over to wait.

Unfortunately, when he saw me go by he had to wait for a long line of traffic, so I ended up several blocks ahead of him. Despairing of losing my way, I pulled over and waited. Then I saw him go by and nervously waited for a break in traffic to get back on the road. By that time, of course, he was again several blocks ahead. We leap-frogged in this manner until we reached the last set of lights on the edge of the city. I breathed a shaky sigh of relief and relaxed my white-knuckled grip on the steering wheel.

"Just follow me." Obeying those three small words is a lot harder than you might think.

Jesus said those same words to His disciples and it meant they had to leave their families, their hometowns, their livelihoods. He never said it would be easy. He said things like, "Anyone who loves his father or mother more than me is not worthy of me; anyone who loves his son or daughter more than me is not worthy of me; and anyone who does not take his cross and follow me is not worthy of me. Whoever finds his life will lose it and whoever loses his life for my sake will find it" (Matthew 10:37-39).

God demands first place in our lives. If we put anything before Him - family, home, career – we will never find our true identity. It is only when we put Him first that we will discover who we really are. And there will be a reward when we do so - our family, home, career will all benefit, and so will we. God has promised that we don't have to do it all alone. He doesn't put us in the driver's seat. He knows how white-knuckled we'd be. So He asks us to let him do the driving. His Spirit guides and directs and gives us the strength to do whatever He asks of us. It's not always easy, but it's the surest way to get to where we want to be.

****

How Do You Spell Relief?

I was humming along in my Austen Mini, minding my own business, when it happened. Flashing lights appeared behind me. I wasn't speeding. I wasn't driving erratically. I knew that section of the Alaska Highway well and was taking care on the tight turns and steep descents. So why, when I saw the flashing lights of the police car, did I feel instantly guilty?

I pulled over immediately. My hands shook as I dug out my drivers license, insurance and registration, even though I knew everything was in order. When the officer asked where I was going, I answered him in barely a whisper. When he handed back my papers, smiled and told me to drive carefully, I sank into the seat with relief. As he walked away, I wanted to shout, "I'm not guilty of anything!" But I kept quiet and watched the cruiser glide by.

Are you smiling? Been there, done that? I've talked to a lot of people who have had similar experiences, and wondered why. Why do we sometimes feel guilty when we know we are innocent? Perhaps it's because, deep inside, we know we aren't so squeaky clean. We have stepped on that gas pedal just a little too hard on occasion. Maybe we have failed to come to a complete stop at an intersection, or parked illegally a time or two. We're all culpable, though we claim absolute innocence. We all want to shout, "I'm not guilty!" But we know we are.

We react the same way when we are faced with a small but extremely unpopular little word - sin. We want to deny our guilt. We mentally list all our good points, all our good deeds. Then we look at some of the "sinners" around us and we're comforted. But denial doesn't change the truth. We are guilty as charged. None of us, not one, has achieved the perfection in body, mind or soul that God intends us to own. We all fall short of that standard.

Fortunately, the Bible supplies us with a big BUT. It's found in Colossians 1:22, "BUT now he has reconciled you by Christ's physical body through death to present you holy in his sight, without blemish and free from accusation." What a relief! Knowing how guilty I am, I can count on Jesus to wipe it all away before God glances my way. I can know that not only will I not *feel* guilty when I come into His presence, I won't *be* guilty. All the falling short won't matter then, because I'll be perfect in body, mind and soul, entirely acceptable to a holy God. What an astounding truth! Jesus has paid the price, done the time, taken the hit. I've been reconciled, redeemed, restored, all because I said yes to Jesus. That's the Gospel, the good news. That's how I spell relief!

****

A Shovel on the Highway

Driving the highway between my home and a near-by city is something that has become a regular and rather boring experience. I usually read when my husband drives, but when I have to do the driving I keep myself awake by watching for anything interesting on the side of the road.

One day I saw something that made me chuckle. A snow shovel was stuck upright out of a rather high snow bank. We'd had a lot of snow that week, but there was no sign that a vehicle had been stuck in the ditch. Seeing the shovel made me wonder what happened to the person who owned it. And what was he trying to do with it? The idea of trying to shovel the highway with such a small tool was ludicrous. I began to picture someone attempting such a feat, becoming overwhelmed and exhausted and in frustration abandoning the shovel in the bank.

Whatever had happened, that shovel kept my mind occupied all the way to the city. It made me think of how we, in our own strength try to do the Lord's work. So many of us are attempting what is comparable to clearing a highway with a snow shovel! There is no way we can do it.

The Lord cautioned his disciples about this after his resurrection. He told them, "wait for the gift my Father promised, which you have heard me speak about. For John baptized with water, but in a few days you will be baptized with the Holy Spirit" (Acts 1:4,5). Jesus knew they could never accomplish the things He was about to ask of them unless they had the Holy Spirit to help them. He said, "But you will receive power when the Holy Spirit comes on you; and you will be my witnesses in Jerusalem and in all Judea and Samaria and to the ends of the earth" (Acts 1:8).

Trying to clear a highway with a snow shovel is an impossible task. "But with God, all things are possible" (Matt.19:26). With God, we can do what seems impossible without becoming overwhelmed or exhausted. The key is to rely on His Spirit, His strength and to tune in to what God is doing. When we see and recognize His hand at work, our load is instantly lighter and we are energized to go on.

When we allow the Spirit to work through us we are encouraged by what He does and revitalized for the work.

****

Signposts and Other Living Things

I once lived in a town with no street signs. At first that was a problem, because I didn't know the history of the people. Someone would invite me over and describe where they lived by telling me whose house it used to be, or whose house it was near: "It used to be Old Pete's place. Oh. You didn't know Old Pete. Do you know Joe's house? Hmm...well, it's around the corner from Blackfoot John's place, you know, where Crazy Cathy used to live...."

It took a while to find my way. Eventually, I learned about the people and the events which had distinguished them and the houses where they lived. Then the town council decided it was time to put up some signs. They looked good. I found out Old Pete had lived on the corner of 6th and Front Streets. For the first while, nobody referred to his place that way. They still said, "It's around the corner from Blackfoot John's." Then winter came. They discovered the signs stood just a little too far into the street. The snow plough operators weren't used to them being there. By spring they weren't. The next summer the town put a few back up, but it was a heavy snow that winter and by spring the signs had disappeared again. Town council decided to stop wasting money and left the streets unsigned.

Years later, the town had an influx of tourists. Strangers flooded in every summer. I knew the place was becoming home when I found myself giving directions like: "It's right behind the house where Grizzly Jack used to live." Soon, tourists and locals were frustrated with the inefficiency. Then the town invested in some heavy metal posts topped by large numbered signs, set firmly on the corners well back from the path of snow ploughs and other large objects. The locals still used the "historical" method among themselves, but when a stranger asked directions, the signs made life easier. I was a bit sad when they became, more and more, the only way people gave directions. Before the signs went up, the places were known by the people who had lived there. The people were the essential ingredient.

In Hebrews 11, there is a long list of people. The writer lays out a pattern of faith from one generation to the next, using the stories of the lives of those gone by. It is a pattern we would do well to imitate. God's glory is manifest in the stories of His people, those who have lived and are living lives of faith. We should all know them. There's a great book about them, called the Bible. It's a portrait of the face of God, evidenced in the lives of His people. Hebrews 11 is a good place to start. Why not read it today? (If you need one, come see me. I live in Jackie and Darren's old house!)

****

A Travelers' Advisory

I rolled over in bed and listened to the radio. "White-out conditions on Highway #2," the announcer said. I rolled back under the covers. I really didn't want to get up anyway. I heard my husband finish shaving in the bathroom and perked up enough to tell him what the radio had said. "Looks like we'll be staying home, eh?"

Spence glanced at his watch. "Well, I'll call the driver and see what he thinks." A few minutes later Spence was shaking me awake again. "Looks like we're going to go for it. Are you coming?"

I should have followed my instincts – those warning lights going off in my brain that kept repeating the weatherman's words. But I'm not one to miss anything, so off we went to meet the ten others who had planned to travel with us. After a few minutes of consultation, it was decided to ignore the warning on the radio. "They always exaggerate," "Yeah, it can't be that bad." We piled into the van and headed south on Highway #2.

The first twenty kilometers were fine. A skiff of snow blew across the road, the small flakes melting as they hit the windshield. Our mood was jovial as we sipped our coffee and talked with anticipation about the seminar we were going to attend. Just south of Red Deer the flakes started getting bigger. The road started getting icier. The van started slowing down. It wasn't long before the visibility was zero and we were all peering out, looking for an exit. We saw several vehicles crunched into each other and many more half buried in snow in the ditches on both sides. Warning lights were flashing in my brain again – in big neon letters – GET OFF THIS ROAD!

It was more than an hour before we were able to do so, pulling into a town with no power, no open restaurants, no empty motel rooms. We gathered with many others in a motel lobby as a policeman told us to be prepared to stay a while. I looked around at the crowd and wondered why we had all ignored the warning. It had been clear. It was from a reliable source. Yet we chose to believe in our own indestructibility, our own resources.

The writer of Hebrews 12:25-29 says, "See to it that you do not refuse him who speaks. If they did not escape when they refused him who warned them on earth, how much less will we, if we turn away from him who warns us from heaven? ... for our God is a consuming fire."

We have been warned. God will not be patient forever. He sent His Son to guide us back to Him, to warn us away from the road that leads to death. Are you ignoring the warning? You may end up in a place with no power, no nourishment, no place to rest. Heed the warning now, before it's too late.

****

An Unusual Rescue

If we had heard a weather forecast, we might have stayed home. It was only about thirty-five degrees below zero when we headed to town, but by the time we came out of a meeting, close to midnight, it had dropped to minus sixty-five. Our truck would not start. Neither would the other vehicles parked outside.

As I watched from the warmth of the doorway, my husband and a few friends donned some unusual head gear and hovered over the one truck they thought might rise to the occasion. Their head gear, hats woven of warm Alpaca wool, had tall peaks with tassels on the ends and long tapered ear flaps that bobbed with each step. They made the guys look a lot like Santa's elves. None of them realized how comical they looked, as they scurried around the truck, trying to get it to start. Someone produced a propane torch to heat the oil pan. Someone else produced a tarp to cover the hood. Then we all huddled in the doorway, hoping for success. We cheered when the motor roared to life before catching on fire!

As we crammed into the cab for the trip home, the guys left their hats on, still oblivious to how they looked. We had only gone a few miles when we saw a faint light. It burned for a few moments, then died. We leaned forward as it appeared again, directly ahead. Our driver slowed down as we got closer. The dim light flashed one more time and we realized it was a truck in the middle of the road. All of us piled out as we pulled to the side to investigate.

The truck door opened and a young woman peered out. Her lips were blue, her bare hands, wrapped around a small kitten, were white with frost bite. She tried to swing her legs out but needed help. When she stood up, her feet, clad only in running shoes, wouldn't move. As the men lifted her into the warm vehicle, I noticed she looked at them with an odd expression. It wasn't until later we discovered she thought she was hallucinating. She didn't expect to be rescued by a band of Santa's elves!

Psalm 118:5 says, "In my distress I prayed to the Lord and the Lord answered me and rescued me."

Rescue. In the nick of time. If we hadn't been on the road that night, that young woman would have died. I don't know if she prayed, but, in desperate situations, most people do.

Unfortunately, most of us don't recognize we are just such in a desperate place when we are without God. We depend on things like trucks with heaters, refusing to believe they might break down in the worst places at the worst times. We think we're safe, we're okay, when in reality we're on the brink of disaster. God is in the rescue business and we all need to be rescued.

****

When The Road Disappears

We were facing that long road once again. We knew every bend, every straight stretch and every dangerous descent. The Alaska Highway, all 1,500 hundred miles of it, was no stranger. We sipped coffee in a diner and chatted with a local man. "Why don't you try that new road?" he suggested. "They say it's straighter so it's gotta be shorter."

Spence's ears perked up. "New road?"

"Yeah, it heads north near Hazelton. "Can't miss it."

We checked the map. There was no sign of a road heading north from New Hazelton, but the local "expert" assured us the map was too old and the road too new.

"It's there all right. Been on it myself."

Anxious to avoid the other route, we decided to take the risk and headed for the rugged countryside of northern British Columbia. We found the highway, and it did indeed look good. In fact, for the first fifty kilometers, the fresh pavement and beautiful scenery made us bless the man in the diner. Then the pavement ended. We had expected that. After all, it was a new road. The gravel was well graded for about the next twenty kilometers. Then the highway narrowed and it was obvious the grader had quit. Then the road looked more like a driveway than a highway. Then it happened. We rounded a bend and the road disappeared.

Huge machinery attempted to level piles of rubble before us. A flagman appeared, radio in hand as he stared at us, shook his head and turned back to the earthmovers. Spence pressed the accelerator and eased the truck forward.

The flagman rushed over. "Where do you think you're going?" he shouted.

"Whitehorse," Spence shouted back.

"There's thirty klicks of rubble between here and the next section," the flagman warned, shifted his hard hat and added, "But there's no blasting today."

Spence patted the dash of our old '66 GMC. "She'll get us through."

The man waved his flag with a flourish and we headed off. It took us several hours to negotiate those thirty kilometers, but eventually we found the other end of the road and celebrated our victory with relief. We'd made it! Our old truck had proven itself again.

Sometimes tragedy strikes and the road ahead seems filled with nothing but rubble. Despair lies just around the next bend. Yet there is hope and a promise. James 1:12 says, "Blessed is the man who perseveres under trial, because when he has stood the test, he will receive the crown of life that God has promised to those who love Him." James uses a well known example – "You have heard of Job's perseverance and have seen what the Lord finally brought about. The Lord is full of compassion and mercy" (Jas.5:11).

Facing a road full of obstacles gives us an opportunity to trust God. Keep moving forward and He'll get you through. He's much more trustworthy than an old '66 GMC.

****

3 ON VACATION

A Confident Word On a High Ridge

"Now we have a decision to make." I shifted in my saddle to look at our trail guide as he continued. "We can go back the way we came up, or we can follow this ridge to the other side of that mountain."

The ride to the top of the highest peak in the range had been great. The view was spectacular, and we were all feeling a bit "high." We opted for the more adventurous route. Our guide led the way onto the narrow ridge. I tried not to tense up as I glanced down. The strip of dirt was just wide enough for the animals to plant their feet. Both sides fell away steeply. I watched the animal in front of me shiver and kick at horse flies that materialized out of nowhere. I began to think we had made the wrong decision. We were in a precarious place and the potential for disaster very real.

Our guide turned and said, "By the way, you're the first woman I've taken across this ridge. How ya doin'?"

I sat straight and answered, "I'm fine!"

We reached the end of the ridge and breathed easier as the trail wound around the face of the mountain. Eventually a solid trail took us down the mountain, across a river and finally back to the campsite. We were weary but exhilarated. We had accepted a challenge and it had come out well. We would have stories to tell and memories to cherish.

As I looked back at the experience, I remembered that moment when our guide had expressed his confidence in me. I realized he was probably more confident of my horse's surefootedness than of my riding ability, but I also realized his words had inspired me. After all, he was one of the best. If he thought I could do it, then I was sure I could. From that moment I relaxed and somehow the danger didn't seem quite so unnerving.

When we find ourselves in precarious places in life, we can rely on a Guide who has complete confidence in us. He knows He has given us everything we need to get through - access to His Father, (God), a spiritual Counselor,(The Holy Spirit), brothers and sisters to talk to and pray with,(Christian friends), a family to care for us, (our churches) and most of all, His own strength and love. We, therefore, are encouraged.

Psalm 27:3 says, "Though an army besiege me, my

heart will not fear; though war break out against me, even then will I be confident."

We can be sure God is going to get us to our destination. Jesus is our guide, the One who expresses His love and confidence in us. He knows we can accomplish our life's tasks because He will be there leading the way, walking with us. Believe Him. He's the best trail guide there is.

****

A Landmark to Set our Bearings Straight

When we pulled into Dawson City at one a.m., I strained to see something familiar. The bus squealed to a stop and we stepped out into a biting Yukon wind, our boots thudding on the damp boardwalk. The leap onto the street sent sprays of mud over my new hikers as I continued to peer around. By the light of a single street lamp, I realized I was standing in front of Dawson's most famous hotel. The store across the street had the same massive carved doors I remembered, though the sign above them had changed. A Husky stopped to stare and bark at us. I relaxed. This was familiar.

As I set out the next day through the town where I'd once lived, it became obvious things had changed. The northern community is known for moving its buildings around (a local joke is, "Dawson, the city of no fixed address"). So I found myself looking for landmarks to set my bearings straight. The post office is still on 5th Ave., the Downtown Hotel still dominates its corner and the old bank is still the only building sitting on the south bank of the Yukon River. By keeping the familiar in mind, I was able to make my way around without any trouble. The familiar places stirred memories long forgotten, bringing people to mind as I remembered the good times and the bad. Landmarks. Without them we'd be lost.

Throughout the Old Testament the Israelites built landmarks and altars to help them remember not only the lay of the land but the blessings of their God. Each time God showed Himself to them in some way, they built an altar to Him and gave that place a name. The people could trace their history by referring to these places. When they were firmly established in Jerusalem they built their most permanent altar, the Temple, where they worshiped and offered sacrifices to atone for their sins. It was a monument to memory and to the future.

When Jesus came He changed that. No longer was it necessary to remember God in that way. God had presented Himself to them and became a new landmark for all mankind. Hebrews 13:15 says, "Through Jesus, therefore, let us continually offer to

God a sacrifice of praise - the fruit of lips that confess his name." Hebrews 13:10 says, "we have an altar..." That altar is Jesus, Himself.

Our physical landmarks are important, even today. We build monuments and install plaques. We re-name streets and create parks to honor those of importance. Our landmarks tell us where we've been and point the way to where we should go. Jesus is our spiritual landmark. He reveals where we've been, where we need to go, and how to get there. Keep your eye on Him and you'll set your bearings straight.

****

"Ain't No Journey Hopeless"

In the film, *Hurricane*, there's a thread that I'm sure warms the heart of every writer. A young man, whose life is full of distress, picks a book from a bin at a second-hand store and takes it home. The book not only changes his life, but, because he is moved to connect with its author, in prison for a crime he did not commit, it changes the writer's life too. When the young man and the writer meet, Hurricane Carter asks him, "Do you think it was an accident you picked up my book?" Hurricane implies it was not. He implies it was in the plan. The book was meant for that young man. It set him on a path, a journey designed for him, a journey during which he would find what he needed, to live.

God often works that way. He puts things and people in our path, like books on the top of bins in second-hand stores, which give us what we need for that time in our lives. Some years ago, it happened to me. My family and I had enjoyed a wonderful vacation horseback riding in the mountains. We were on our way home and stopped to visit friends and attend their church. As we walked in we were handed a bulletin with a picture of a beautiful mountain peak on the cover. The pastor's sermon was about taking what you learn on the spiritual mountain top experiences and applying them to times in your life when you are in that opposite place, the dark lonely valleys. He didn't preach theory, but used real-life stories to illustrate what he meant. When we returned home that night, the phone rang. It was my mother telling me my dad had died early that day.

I'm sure the pastor of that church had no idea what I would go through in the next hours and days after his sermon. I'm sure he did not realize he was picking all those stories for me, and likely for others who heard him. But I believe that is exactly what happened. I was able to draw on that sermon, on those stories, and the stories in the Bible, to regain my balance, my sense of identity, and my hope.

A friend recently sent me this wonderful quote – "..And in Bible-story journeys, ain't no journey hopeless. Everybody find what they supposed to find..." (from *"Sounder"* by William H. Armstrong.) Talk to anyone who reads the Bible regularly and they will tell you that statement is more than true. Hebrews 4:12 says, "For the word of God is living and active. Sharper than any double edged sword, it penetrates even to dividing soul and spirit, joints and marrow..."

The Bible story journeys are meant for each and every one of us. They will provide the hope, the joy, and sometimes just the dogged determination we need to keep going on the path we are meant to follow.

****

Angels in the Badlands

Just after we found our seats in the bleachers, I could feel perspiration trickling its way down my back. The sun was high and blazing. The only shade was a narrow strip along one wall of the stage where a crowd lingered, waiting for the call signaling the start of the Badlands Passion Play. I was prepared for the heat, with two containers of water and a broad-brimmed hat.

It was my lack of tissues that worried me. I'd anticipated needing them. I just hadn't realized it would happen before the performance began. The program for the play describes this time as the pre-show. Actors dressed as temple guards and high priests perform their duties, women cry out for passers-by to inspect their wares in the market. Children dash about and centurions patrol on horse-back. My eyes roamed from scene to scene, fascinated by the portrayal of life during the time of Christ.

Then something caught my eye: a movement high on a hill behind the set. Figures in white began to sway. Ministering angels. Seeing them high above the bustle below stirred something deep within me. At the time, I did not understand what it was. I just knew I couldn't look at them without weeping.

I believe in angels. I believe they are God's creation, separate and distinct from human beings, "ministering spirits sent to serve those who will inherit salvation" (Hebrews 1:14). However, I had not thought of them, before that day, in terms of expressing God's love. Throughout the production they ministered, portraying the presence of God in the midst of an often oppressive reality, by the simple movement of their bodies, their arms and hands. Their reaching out, their hovering, spoke of the longing of God to minister to us, to love us.

The one movement that broke my resolve to keep the tears back happened as Jesus hung on the cross. As he called out those agonizing words, "Eloi, Eloi, lama sabachthani - My God, my God, why have you forsaken me?" The angels turned their backs to Him. That movement, above all, spoke of the shocking love of God, that He would forsake His son for our sake. For my sake. I wept again as the angel announced His resurrection, and again when they danced as He embraced His friends who thought Him dead.

There's an old saying, that seeing is believing, and I pray that it's true. I pray that those who have thought of Jesus only as an historical figure might be touched by something deeper as they watch the portrayal of His life by actors under a blazing sun. I pray they'll be touched by His love as they watch the angels in the Alberta Badlands.

****

An Appreciation for Light

We knew we were headed for an adventure. Nine of us were loaded up in an old van, our bones jarred by a road which deteriorated quickly into little more than pot holes joined together to form a goat path. Our eyes widened a little more every time we forded one of the thirteen rivers slashing across it. The dense Papua New Guinean jungle crowded close at some points, opened out into fields of elephant grass at others, and every now and then, allowed a panorama of the sea. Eventually we arrived at our destination, a small village clinging to a sandy spit reaching out into the ocean. People flocked out of their homes as the word spread that there were "dim-dims" (white people) in their village.

We had arranged for a boat to meet us there, but after two hours of waiting, concluded it was not going to arrive, and accepted the offer of a guide to some caves nearby. After an hour of hacking along a trail that slowly got steeper and steeper, our guide pointed with his machete. We could see a large indentation in the mountain, a black hole about the size of a one-story house. The climb up wasn't easy, but we managed and soon arrived at the lip of the cave. The climb down into it was even more of a challenge, our guide training his flashlight at the ground as we descended one by one.

When we were all assembled he shifted the light, fanning it into the cavern beyond. The shock of what we saw there still lingers with me. Piles of skulls, eye sockets seeming to move in the eerie glow of the flashlight, stared back at us. Our guide said this was a small group, that other caverns were more full. There were hundreds, perhaps even thousands of skulls and skeletons lying in the bowels of the mountain. Our guide admitted his grandfather had been one of those who came here to devour his victims.

In silence, we followed as he led us further into the cave, pointing out more piles of skulls as we went. Finally, he said we had to decide which direction to go, either turn back and descend the mountain the same way we had come, or continue on into the caves, which eventually opened at a lower point on the other side. After checking to make sure he really knew how to get through, the group decided to carry on. The further we went, the deeper the darkness, the more narrow the passageways. At times we had to squeeze around stalagmites and crawl under overhangs. Several times our guide would lead one or two of us through, then leave us to go back for the others, taking the only light with him. He was never gone for long, but the minutes seemed liked hours as we stood in complete and utter darkness.

It was with great relief we eventually saw an opening and felt the intense tropical sun pouring through the exit. Stepping out into the humid heat and lushness of the rainforest was like being literally raised from a grave. The words of Jesus in Matthew 4:16, had never been more powerful: "the people living in darkness have seen a great light; on those living in the land of the shadow of death a light has dawned," and in John 12:46 - "I have come into the world as a light, so that no one who believes in me should stay in darkness."

Having just experienced both a real and a deadly darkness, the words filled us with a thankfulness for

His light. Papua New Guinea was once a "land in the shadow of death," but we did not have to worry that our guide was taking us to those caves to murder and consume us, (though there were moments I did pray he was trustworthy!) We did not have to fear being left in that utterly dark place. The light of Christ was within us. He "turns my darkness into light" (Psalm 18:28). His light is available to us all, even in the darkest of places.

****

Fear Factor

It was a beautiful summer day. My friend Lynn and I chatted as we strolled among groups of other people heading for one of B.C.'s main tourist attractions. I had glanced at the brochure Lynn showed me the day before and had a moment of hesitation when I saw the picture. Since falling on the cliffs on Lake Superior the year before, I had developed a fear of heights, but I listened as Lynn read the details in the brochure and was confident I would have no problem. We rounded the bend in the path and there it was, The Capilano Suspension Bridge. I watched as a young boy ran out onto it and jumped up and down. The bridge bounced and swayed. I hesitated. Lynn stepped boldly out and was almost half way across before she realized I wasn't behind her. She waved me on. I took a deep breath and stepped onto the creaking boards.

I walked about two meters. Then that same young boy ran onto the bridge from the opposite end and jumped up and down again. The bridge swayed and buckled. I froze. My hands seemed glued to the steel cables, my feet would not move and my eyes would not focus on anything but the roaring Capilano River, 250 feet below. I had never had a panic attack before. I didn't know what was happening to me, but I knew I could not move, neither forward nor back. I heard Lynn calling from the far side of the gorge, but I could not turn my head away from the river below.

Then I felt Lynn's hand on mine. She urged me to look at her, and I finally pulled my eyes away from the gorge. Then I allowed her to remove one of my hands from the steel cable. I shifted my feet as she led me back toward the closest side of the gorge.

I knew the statistics about the bridge – that the cables were encased in thirteen tons of concrete at both ends. I knew that thousands of people had walked across it safely. But fear blocked all reason and left me paralyzed. Fear. It can destroy all sense of logic and reason.

When we are in a place of extreme stress, fear can be a powerful factor. Like that day on that bridge, it can keep us from moving forward. At such times it's good to have a friend like Lynn, one who will gently guide and lead us back to a place where we feel safe. Jesus is standing beside us, ready to be that friend.

Through the prophet Isaiah, He says – "So do not fear, for I am with you; do not be dismayed, for I am your God. I will strengthen you and help you; I will uphold you with my righteous right hand" (Isaiah 41:10). Listen for His voice. Focus on Him, and the fear will be gone.

****

If Life Were Like That ...

A Ruth Buzy look-alike sits in a teller's booth at the entrance to an amusement park. A large crowd stands before her. She smiles broadly and tells them this is their lucky day because ... and she rhymes off all those who will be allowed into the park free that day: fathers, mothers and children, pregnant women, and women who want to be pregnant, people with no hair and people with hair. The list goes on and on and it becomes obvious that everyone will get in free. The people smile and look at one another with surprise. Can this be true?

Then the narrator says, "If life were like that, you wouldn't need (a well-know credit card)." The inference is, of course, that everyone needs that credit card because in the real world the price has to be paid. That's a reality no one would argue with. We all know sayings like, 'You don't get something for nothing,' and 'You get what you pay for.' No one argues with the logic. Experience bears it out time and again. We all know the price has to be paid.

Imagine St. Peter at the gates to heaven. He's looking out at the multitudes that have died that day. He smiles broadly and lists all those who will get in free. It becomes obvious to the crowd that the list includes everyone. They look at one another with surprise. Can it be true?

Then they hear the voice of their Heavenly Father. "If salvation were like that, you wouldn't need my Son." If everyone gets in free, the torture and death of Jesus are irrelevant. If everyone gets in free, why did Jesus bother? Why was it he "humbled himself and became obedient to death – even death on a cross!" (Philippians 2:8) Why did he pay the price with his own blood, if the cost of admission was going to be waived at the gate?

The reality is, the price of our sin must be paid. We cannot remain in the presence of God with sin on our souls. The good news is that we have all been "bought at a price" (1 Corinthians 6:20). The price was the blood of Jesus, the Son of God. He was the only one who could pay it, the only one who could free us from the debt.

Some day we will be ushered into the presence of our Heavenly Father and we will need to present a means of payment in order to stay with Him. We can't use our credit card – the shiny gold kind won't work, neither will the platinum. Only the name of Jesus on our lips and His Spirit in our hearts will suffice. Only the shadow of His righteousness covering our sin will open that gate. We all know the price has to be paid. Do you have the means?

****

The Longings of Our Hearts

Watching salmon at the North Fork of the Klondike River was a lot like watching fireworks. Although we expected each explosion, we still let out an exclamation of appreciation. The salmon would erupt, flashing, gleaming with pure energy, huge orange and red bodies bursting out of the water. The dam was alive with them, the swift water no match for their instinctual race to spawn.

We exclaimed as each one appeared, cheering them on, because we wanted them to win, to fling their bodies high and hard enough to escape the incessant pull of that water. We knew somehow they would do it and the cycle of life would continue, though many would die in the process. At the time I did not attribute any kind of philosophical meaning to our cheers, passionate as they were. I just knew we wanted the fish to win.

Now, however, I wonder why. Why were we so passionate about those slimy, bug-eyed creatures who could neither change their course nor articulate the reasons for their mad dash up that falls? Perhaps it was a sense of their fight being part of ours, their conquest of those unreasonable odds, somehow tied to our battle to do the same. We, too, are driven forward by unseen forces. The drive to succeed, the drive to create, to surround ourselves with love, beauty, peace and order, all of these lie deep in our being.

At the core of the salmon's fight upriver is the instinct for survival. At the core of our need for those things which captivate us, is the need to know our creator.

We fight toward peace, order, beauty, love and yes, even success in our lives, because these are part of the character of God. And, at our core, we know we need Him. We need Him as desperately as those salmon need to make it to their spawning grounds.

Somewhere along the way, however, we confuse that need with the object of the race. We substitute the love, order, success, for the One who ordained that they exist. And we die a slow spiritual death. Just as surely as those salmon die on their journey, their very flesh disintegrating, so we will die, if we never reach the source of our longings.

Though we are driven to satisfy them, the yearnings of our hearts can never be satiated apart from knowing God. Psalm 63:1 says, "O God... my soul thirsts for you, my body longs for you, in a dry and weary land where there is no water."

It is through a relationship with the Creator, who draws us through those yearnings, that we understand them and truly understand ourselves.

Psalm 63 continues, "My soul will be satisfied as with the richest of foods; with singing lips my mouth will praise you." (v.5)

Are you wearing yourself out, like a salmon in a waterfall, trying to satisfy the longings of your heart? Turn to the One whose essence is love, peace, order and beauty. You will be satisfied.

****

A Rubber Raft, a Mighty River, the Book of Job

It was a foolish thing to do and I should have known

better, but the stress in my life at the time, plus a huge dollop of youthful obstinacy, blinded my better judgment. I set off, alone on the Yukon River, in a small rubber raft. My destination was a friend's cabin somewhere downstream. I'd never been there but I put the thought of missing it out of my mind, even though going by it would mean I'd be on my way to Alaska. The raft was just big enough for me to stretch out - my legs touched the other end without any effort. There was only one paddle, so the raft rotated instead of going straight. The fact that I was extremely ill prepared to be alone on such a vast river didn't occur to me until I was a few miles from anywhere, drifting in circles in the middle of it. The Yukon is wide and cold. Sitting there alone I remembered someone saying if you fell in you'd have two minutes or less before the cold shocked your body into death. I tried not to think about it.

I was out there because I was about to change the course of my life. Though I did not want to make that decision, I felt there was no choice. I felt trapped and I was angry. Until I found myself in the middle of the Yukon River. The country around me was vast. I knew if I pointed in any direction, I could probably count on one hand the number of people who might be out there. I knew it would take several hands and feet to count the Grizzlies. I watched the weather sweep over the hills, clouds unloading their burden of moisture into the valleys and moving on. I watched rainbows arch over me and felt the breeze like a gentle kiss smelling of sweet poplar. Though I realized the country was formidable, I had a deep sense of something being in control. I was a small dot in a tiny gray raft. Suddenly my huge decision seemed almost comically insignificant.

Sometimes it's hard to keep things in the right perspective. We get tangled up in our lives. We feel trapped and angry with God. That's when it's good to take a step out of our normal environment and realize who is in control. In the vastness of the universe, God is the One whose voice is like the refreshing rains and His breath like a breeze carrying sweet fragrances. It is God who puts the rainbows in the sky. Do you need some perspective? Read Job chapters 38 and 39. God asks a series of questions, like, "Where were you when I laid the foundations of the earth?" (Job 38: 4). Reading those two chapters is like sitting in a tiny rubber raft in the middle of the Yukon River. Your perspective changes when you realize who is in control.

By the way, I made it to my friends' cabin without meeting any grizzlies along the way.

****

The Rest of The Story

When I stepped into that raft and left the shore I heard a strange hissing noise and almost panicked. Was there a leak in the side? I checked for bubbles but could see none. The raft seemed to be holding its shape. As the current took me quickly out into the deepest part of the river, I realized what I was hearing was the sound of silt hitting rubber. A few miles down river I heard another sound. It seemed to be getting louder with each minute. It sounded like a waterfall. My heart raced again, as I doubted my friends' information about the lack of white water on this stretch of the Yukon. When the sound was almost as deafening as a freight train, with no white water in site, I began to look for another explanation. As the raft was sucked into a small whirlpool at the base of a cliff, I found the answer. Erosion. The water had gouged a cave into the rock, forming an effective sound chamber for the swirling eddies. The sound echoed out over the water. A few strong strokes with the paddle took me past it.

The rest of the trip consisted of trying to find an over-night camping spot where there was no bear sign, then some hard paddling the next day to maneuver the raft to the other side of the river. Once I reached that side I searched for the small island at the mouth of a creek, where my friends lived. After an unplanned swim, which left my legs so numb I couldn't stand, I arrived at my destination, greatly relieved.

It was not until I did another river trip that I realized how stressful that first foray had been. The second trip was in a sturdy canoe, in the company of friends with strong arms. We had more food than we needed and protection against Grizzlies (just in case). That second trip was peaceful and full of laughter.

Going through life is sometimes like drifting down a river. We're looking for something but we're not sure exactly what or where it is. There is only one certainty – there will be dangers, real and imagined. We'll anticipate white water but find only noise; we'll see bear sign, maybe even be mauled a time or two; we will find ourselves swimming frantically and reach the shore just in time. Life is full of struggles and adventures. How we prepare for them determines how we will live. Fear and anxiety can plague us or peace and joy can be our mainstay.

Jesus is the only source for the latter. He is like those friends with strong arms. As the Prophet Isaiah declares, "You will keep in perfect peace him whose mind is steadfast, because he trusts in You" (Isaiah 26:3). Life can be a joyful journey instead of a struggle to survive when we invite Jesus to go with us.

*****

Small Miracles

When I found out we had to make a four and a half hour trek through the jungles of the Sepik area of Papua New Guinea, I started praying. Then I talked to one of my co-workers, Gloria, who had done it the year before. She told me it had taken her group six and a half hours to do the trek, slogging through knee deep muck most of the way. The trails there are often made of short logs laid across the path. When it rains, these float and become very slimy and difficult to walk on, but to step off means to sink deep into the muck. Every now and then, my friend explained, it's advisable to stop to pull the leaches off. The photos she showed me were not encouraging.

After talking to Gloria I prayed more fervently. I prayed for a helicopter! Realizing that might be a bit unrealistic, I prayed for a week without rain. That too, in the rainforests of PNG, is like praying for a miracle. The closer we got to the day of the walk, the more I dreaded it. While in the village, we learned there had been torrential rains in the next valley. I prayed harder. The morning we had to leave, I listened for the whap whap whap whap of helicopter rotors, but none were heard. There was no other way, but to put on my best footgear and follow our guide.

The trek turned out to be a delight. Our guide

walked at my slow pace and the trail was dry! Every now and then, our guide would grin at me and point out spots that were often waist deep in slime, or sections usually under water. He'd grin and say, "Oh, Mama, yu amamas, tru, a? ren i no kam. - Oh, Mrs., you are very happy, eh? The rain did not come." He was right - I was very happy, not just because the rains hadn't come, but because I knew who had kept them at bay. God had kept the rains away. He kept them away until the day after we left - then a torrential downpour flooded that valley. The rivers and ravines we had crossed without problems were impassable for days.

That day in the jungle of Papua New Guinea was a gift from the hand of God to me. How many times to we miss His gifts? How dangerously we tread when we ignore them and their source. Romans 1 warns that the wrath of God will come to those who do not acknowledge God – "since what may be known about God is plain to them, because God has made it plain to them.... For although they knew God, they neither glorified him as god, nor gave thanks to him, but their thinking became futile and their foolish hearts were darkened" (Romans 1:19 & 21).

Has God revealed Himself to you? Have you received gifts from His hand? Acknowledge them. Acknowledge Him. Be Thankful.

****

Are We Just Touring a Cathedral?

You could not stand before the building without looking up. It was one of those massive European cathedrals, built in the age of religious fervor, whose architects seemed to have one message - look up, look way up. Every line of the structure flowed toward heaven.

As I melted into the stream of people entering the church, I could imagine the throngs who, centuries ago, crowded into this cathedral to hear God's word. It did not take long for that illusion to disappear. A tour guide with a voice like a megaphone began his litany of historical facts: how long it took to build the structure; where the stone was quarried and how many men it took to finish the job; who commissioned and who designed the works of art.

As we entered the sanctuary, the atmosphere changed as the building opened into the massive open area supported by pillars and framed in stained glass. For a moment I had the sense of history again, a sense of understanding the purpose for this edifice. The tour guide's voice again broke through as he began to lead us toward the altar.

It was at that point that I frowned. From the back of the large group, I watched the guide lead the people up a short flight of stairs onto the platform, where a priest was in the midst of celebrating the mass. The megaphone voice was lowered slightly as the group passed behind the altar. I noticed some of the other tourists at least had the courtesy to look sheepish. Caught in the flow, I continued with the crowd, feeling as though we were all participating in a crime. When I think back on that moment, I realize we were.

When I think of it now, I realize we still are. In the presence of our God, we remain aloof. We stand back and gawk, indifferent and unmoved. Like the architects of old, God designed our world to make us turn to Him. He put a yearning in our hearts to worship and made us into His church. He gave us the institution of marriage and entrusts us with children, to teach us about our relationship with Him.

A cartoon once appeared in the pages of many Canadian newspapers. To Canadian baby boomers, it had immediate significance. One of our childhood television heroes, The Friendly Giant, had died. Friendly always began his program with the words "Look up, look way up," as the camera moved up from the toe of his large boot to his smiling face. The newspaper cartoon echoed those words and showed a large hand reaching down toward him.

It is not only in death that God tells us to look up. Romans 1:20 says, "For since the creation of the world, God's invisible qualities - his eternal power and divine nature - have been clearly seen, being understood from what has been made, so that men are without excuse."

All the lines of life say, "Look up, look way up." Isn't it time we did?

****

Travel and What it Does to You

I once returned from a sixteen day trip across the Pacific Ocean. Being on open water for that long eventually gives you good sea legs but when you return you find you also have an inner ear that seems to insist that you are still bobbing and rolling along, days after you have arrived on dry land.

Returning home also comes with the disorienting feeling that you've been away for months instead of days, while the "catching up" adds to the feeling that you really didn't go anywhere at all. Somewhere in between all of that are the memories.

They cling to you, images of tropical jungles and a variety of plant life that is stunning, smells that put you right back in the spot where you bent to sniff that flower, and sounds that make you stop and listen for those brightly coloured birds. Then you realize all of it is now far away and remains only in your mind. But the colours remain vibrant, the sounds crisp and clear.

And then there are the people – the woman you met on the ship's deck who is likely making her last voyage on this earth; the tiny lady with exuberant energy who always wore a hat; the woman from India who remembered your name even though she had only met you once over a week before; the American who kept bumping into you and saying, "oh yeah, you're the writer;" and the girl from Indonesia who served our meals with a smile that lit up the whole room.

All of it adds up to an experience that changes you, a space of time that shifts your attitudes and makes you thankful for the life you lead and all that's in it. I saw fish I could never have imagined existed and the largest Banyan tree in the world that spreads its roots and branches over an entire city block. I felt the steam of a volcano and the rough texture of the land its eruptions created. I laughed at jokes that really only make sense in another language and tried to twist my tongue to make those unfamiliar sounds.

Oh yes, there were a number of "first world problems" - internet access was almost non-existent, the living space was a little cramped and sometimes the coffee wasn't really hot. But life was made more broad, enriched; opinions were challenged and sensations stimulated.

In short, I joined the ranks of the privileged and travelled. And I am thankful.

"Great are the works of the Lord; they are pondered by all who delight in them" (Psalm 111:2).

****

4 FAR AWAY PLACES

Discovering What's Below

My bones were rattled by the constant jarring of bumping over a road that was more potholes than road. My clothes stuck to me as the tropical heat and humidity reached its peak for the day. I was relieved when our driver, Don, pulled off by a small cove and suggested we go for a swim. The scene was like the pictures of a tropical paradise you see in travel magazines, only the waves moved and the palm trees swayed. The kids hit the water first, delighting in the chance to cool down. I waded in slowly, watching as my husband and Don pulled on snorkel masks and fins and swam quickly into deep water. Floating on the surface was enough for me as I let the warm water soothe my jarred bones. But when Spence came back, he found another mask and coaxed me. "You have to see what's under the surface," he insisted.

I finally agreed and allowed him to show me how to snorkel. At first it was interesting but not terribly impressive, but then Spence waved me on and we swam further out. What lay just a few hundred feet from shore was a spectacle of light and color. A coral reef loomed just below the surface, populated by schools of brightly colored fish. They flashed before us, streaks of vibrant blue, yellow and green. The sculptured coral itself was breathtaking. As we all took turns with the snorkels, the delight of what we had seen shone on our faces. It was an experience I will always treasure. As we drove away from the cove that day, I was struck by the fact that I had almost missed it. Content with the surface, I may never have known what was beneath.

Life is similar. We float on the surface, comfortable and content, unaware of the treasures that lie just below. We refuse to make the effort to see and understand a deeper realm, the delight in knowing God. It is there, ours for the taking.

Psalm 36:8-9 says, "They feast on the abundance of your house; you give them drink from your river of delights. For with you is the fountain of life; in your light we see light."

****

A Little Exposure is Good For Us All

I checked my pack one last time: water, sun block, insect repellent, camera. I was ready. Our trek through the rainforest of Papua New Guinea would take about four hours, if the trail was dry. I'd been praying for weeks that it would be, and although we had heard reports of flash floods in the adjacent valley, it looked like my prayers had been answered. The first river we had to ford was low and the winding path through the jungle was relatively easy to manage. I relaxed and began to enjoy the walk. The dense vegetation afforded many opportunities to photograph the lush plant life. The quick flashes of vibrantly coloured birds and butterflies were reasons to keep my camera ready.

As we forded the second river, we were awed by the appearance of a large black Cockatoo, rare in comparison to the common white variety, and the unmistakable sound of a giant hornbill often made my camera shutter click. By the time we reached our destination, I had gone through the entire roll of film and I was excited about the things I managed to capture.

Our flight arrived and we climbed into the small plane. As I twisted around to pull the seatbelt into place, my camera slipped off my knee onto the floor. I was just quick enough to see the back pop open as it landed, exposing the film. Unfortunately, I hadn't yet rewound it. Although I reacted quickly and snapped the case closed again, when the film was developed my worst fear was realized. The roll was entirely blank. Not even one image had survived the exposure to the light.

When we confess our sins to God, we are exposing them to the light of His forgiveness. His forgiveness is complete. Psalm 103:12 says, "As far as the east is from the west, so far has he removed our transgressions from us." "If we confess our sins, he is faithful and just and will forgive us our sins…" (1 John 1:9).

Like film exposed to the light, our sin is blotted out. Why live with it? You can get rid of it forever.

****

Praying with Our Eyes Open

The waitress placed a large bowl of salad in the middle of the table and handed plates all round. Spence and I chatted with our friends for another few moments, while the waitress poured tall glasses of water, then we bowed our heads, closed our eyes and thanked God for the food we were about to eat and the friendship we could enjoy. It was a common blessing, something that is as ordinary to Christians as breathing. As we dished up the salad, our friend Bob said, "We should have prayed like they do in China." My first thought was, how could it be so different? Then Bob explained.

"You can't bow your head over there. You can't close your eyes. When the people say the blessing over a meal, in public, they look at one another as though they were having a normal conversation, but instead of talking to one another, they talk to God." I was amazed at the need for such caution. But Bob assured me it was necessary. "Over there, you pray with your eyes open, in more ways than one."

We can be thankful, here in North America, that we don't have to be afraid to bow our heads and close our eyes in public. But perhaps there is something of value to be learned from the need to do so.

Pray with your eyes open. The phrase has stayed
with me, and it has occurred to me how meaningful
and exciting praying that way could be. Perhaps you've
already done it. Perhaps you stood on the edge of a
mountain and looked out on an unending scene of
beauty and praised God. Or you looked into the eyes
of a new-born baby and gave thanks. Perhaps you
watched the destruction and devastation of war on
T.V. and prayed for peace. Or drove past an accident
on the highway and prayed for those taken away in an
ambulance. Or perhaps you walked down the street
one day and suddenly started praying for everyone you
saw.

Praying with your eyes open. It's not a bad idea, not
a bad habit to cultivate. The Apostle Paul exhorted the
people of Thessalonica to do just that when he said,
"Pray continually" (I Thess.5:17). There are times, of
course, when our praying should be done in a way that
takes us away from the distractions of external things,
but praying with our eyes open will make us aware of
what's really going on around us. It can put us in touch
with what God is doing and make us a part of it. Too
often we miss it. Our eyes are open but we're not
seeing, we're not being touched by what's around us.

That is God's intention, after all, that we be His
servants on this earth, servants who see and respond in

prayer and in action. Pray continually. Pray with your eyes open. Try it. You might get to like it!

****

Peace and Safety in A High Risk Zone

"This is not a safe place." The Australian director of the Pacific Orientation Centre paced the floor like a military drill sergeant, his eyes flashing, scanning to connect with each of us. "Keep your wits about you! Stay alert! You women should never go anywhere alone." I gulped. We were going to live in Papua New Guinea for a full year. The reality of our situation hit and when we were assigned a house in the "high risk" zone of the mission center, I didn't sleep very well. Perhaps that was because we slept with a large baseball bat beside the bed. Our doors were locked day and night, even when we were in the house. When I had to go to the market, I made sure at least one of my neighbors could walk with me. I did not let my children out of my sight.

Then, one night, just as darkness fell, there was a knock on the door. We peered through the window at a young national boy, about sixteen years old. In rapid Melanesian Pidgin he explained he had gotten locked into the center. He was looking for relatives. He wanted to use our phone. My husband told him to stay there and called security. I will never forget the look of terror on that boy's face when the security guards roared up and took him away. I went to bed that night feeling miserable. After a long night praying, I made a decision. I was not going to live like this anymore. It was making a wreck out of me, and it did not honor God.

I made a call to the security office to make it clear the young man on our doorstep had done nothing wrong. I was relieved when they informed me he had been delivered to his relatives, unharmed. Then I walked to the market, alone. I learned the names of the women I bought vegetables from, and lingered to chat with the men selling baskets. They told me about their villages, their children and their gardens. Over time, we grew to know and to love the people. Over time, we learned to value them more than the possessions in our house, temporary things that would eventually be taken from us by the normal progression of life. We learned that being harmed, even being killed, was not to be dreaded so much as living fearfully.

The possibility of violence and danger surrounds us wherever we go. Our only true security lies in knowing God is in control. Psalm 37:3 says, "Trust in the Lord and do good; dwell in the land and enjoy safe pasture." We are able to live as peacefully as sheep grazing in rich grass, no matter where we are, when we know there is a loving Shepherd watching over us. We are able to live lives filled with joy, not fear, when we trust Him and act in ways that honor Him.

****

Language Learning And a Teachable Attitude

My face was beet red. I slouched into my chair with a dismal sigh. My language teacher, having not the slightest inclination to save my damaged pride, was laughing. I managed a weak smile. It was a bit funny. I had just asked him if he wanted his sister in his coffee. When he stopped laughing, he told me the correct phrase. The difference between the word 'sister' and the word 'sugar' was in a single vowel.

Later that afternoon, I despaired again of ever being able to speak Melanesian Pidgin, as another teacher outlined the grammatical structure of the language. I could barely remember English grammar, let alone bend my brain around a language made up of three European lexicons with a few national dialects thrown in for flavor. By the end of that day, my enthusiasm for learning the trade language of Papua New Guinea had vanished. It was then I realized I didn't want to learn it, I just wanted to know how to speak it!

I wanted to be able to communicate with the people we were to live with, so I had to dispel the illusion that I was going to wake up one morning and be fluent in their language. I had to face the fact that I was going to make a lot of mistakes. I was going to be laughed at. I was going to feel dumb and have to continually ask questions. I was going to have to get used to being like a little child.

When I came to terms with that reality, a surprising thing happened. The process became a delight. I looked forward to shopping in the market, learning new names for old vegetables. I relished going to work, so I could learn new expressions and phrases. I loved standing in the middle of a crowd of black faces and just soaking in the sound. Every day was an exciting learning experience.

In Matthew 18, the arrogance of the disciples was showing. They wanted to know which of them would be the greatest in God's kingdom. They must have figured they'd learned enough, and done enough, to merit the favor of their teacher. Jesus says, "I tell you the truth, unless you change and become like little children, you will never enter the kingdom of heaven. Therefore whoever humbles himself like this child is the greatest in the kingdom of heaven" (Matthew 18:3&4).

Like little children, we should delight in learning something new about God every day. With the eagerness of excited young learners, we should stand in His presence and soak Him in. To reach that place we have to acknowledge we don't know it all. We have to be willing to ask questions, to seek answers, to listen. We have to be willing to be like little children, eager to learn.

****

Living There Makes All the Difference

When my husband and I moved to Saskatchewan, we thought we'd moved into a hair dryer. The wind blowing off the prairie was incessant, hot and dry. I remember standing on the back step of our tiny trailer, looking out at the flat stubble-covered land and thinking it was the ugliest, most desolate piece of country I'd ever seen. We lived there for three years and over that time I saw the land transformed as the seasons followed one after the other and my eyes grew accustomed to subtle changes. One day I stood on that same back step, looking out at a waving wheat field and realized how much I was going to miss watching the play of light, the continual shift of clouds and being able to see to forever.

When we first arrived in Papua New Guinea the people all looked alike. For a while I was nervous about going to the market because I was afraid I would not recognize the woman who worked for us. Not buying vegetables from her would have been very rude. When we left Papua New Guinea I sat in the airport and watched the people I'd come to know. I picked out women from the south and men from the islands off the coast. I wondered how I could ever have thought they all looked alike.

There was a time when I thought the Bible contained nothing but myths and rules. I thought it was designed to control people's behavior and restrict their will. Then I started reading it. I was amazed at the history, the wisdom, and most of all the portrait, painted in words, of a man whose life was having a dramatic affect on my own.

Experience changed my mind in Saskatchewan and in Papua New Guinea, as it did with consistent reading of the scriptures. I discovered that in order to know a place and a people, you have to live among them. In order to know God, you have to read His letters to you.

There was a group of people in ancient times who discovered this. They were called the Bereans. The apostle Paul visited them, teaching and preaching about the Messiah. The Bereans "examined the Scriptures every day to see if what Paul said was true" (Acts 17:11).

God has given us a wonderful promise concerning the scriptures. He said, "As the rain and the snow come down from heaven, and do not return to it without watering the earth ... so is my word that goes out from my mouth; It will not return to me empty, but will accomplish what I desire and achieve the purpose for which I sent it" (Isaiah 55:10,11).

There is a way to claim that promise. Living there makes all the difference.

****

Lost in the Jungle?

An interviewer once asked Mother Theresa why she gave her time and energy, indeed her life, in the face of the millions in need. The misery was so pervasive, how could she possibly hope to change it? I found it fascinating that at first she did not understand the question. Her focus was so fixed on the dignity of each human being that even if she could help only one, it was worth her life.

I believe that is the focus of Christ. He says it himself in the story of the lost sheep - the shepherd leaves those who are safe to rescue the one that is lost. In this day of careful economic management, that makes no sense. In terms of profit and loss, you expect to lose a few. In terms of people management, you work with those who are compatible, those who can do the job, those who produce. Those who don't are not considered worth worrying about, let alone hiring. But Jesus isn't running a business, He's dealing with life and death.

I thought about what it would be like to be lost while walking through the jungle in Papua New Guinea. It made me shiver, even in that tropical heat, to think about trying to find my own way in that place. The jungle was thick with hidden dangers - vipers, poisonous spiders and centipedes, sago swamps full of thorns the size of stiletto knives and leaches almost as big. I had no idea which plants were edible and which were deadly. I had no idea where to find fresh water. I had no idea which of the many paths would lead to a safe place. I did know that in only a few short hours darkness would descend and I didn't even want to think about all the things that would come out then! But because I had a guide to lead me, that walk through the jungle was like a stroll in Stanley Park. Well, almost!

Consider one who is lost. He's in a frightening place, full of hidden dangers, unknown paths and lack of food and water, or a place to rest. It's a place of constant stress, with nowhere to turn, no way out. Then the guide shows up. Suddenly there is someone to point out the pitfalls, someone to shine a light on the path, someone to open a door into a warm room with a feast spread out on the table. Imagine the sense of relief as the lost one follows the direction and accepts the hospitality of the rescuer. Imagine the peace.

Are you lost? Do you feel like you're wandering in a jungle with no way out? There's a Guide who died for the chance to find you, to give you relief, peace, life in abundance and hope that is unquenchable. His name is Jesus and He has been looking for you.

****

Memory Lapses

It's a new day! Spring has brought out the gardeners and landscapers. Yards and parks are getting a facelift. The old is torn away and new growth is flourishing. No wonder we all love springtime. Not only are the days warmer but the world around us is being transformed from dull lifeless grey and brown to fresh, vibrant green leaves and floral blooms. Almost overnight, the world has become a colorful place, but the memory of winter is not far away. In this part of the world, we know we'd better enjoy these warm days while we can, because they are all too short. Having lived a significant part of my life in a climate where winter rules, I remember how impossible it was to forget the cold. In the Yukon the summers are made shorter by the fact that you know you have to be busy preparing, because winter is on its way. If your woodpile isn't the size of a mountain when minus sixty hits, you're in big trouble. I used to wonder what it would be like to live in a place where that pressure did not exist, a place where it was summer all the time.

Now I have experienced it, having lived in the southern hemisphere for a time. While in Papua New Guinea, I was amazed at how quickly I was able to forget about winter. Receiving letters from home about snow storms and frigid temperatures only reinforced the sense of distance. Where I was, the flowers were in full bloom and the tropical sun burned my nose if I didn't keep a hat on. Forty below? Not possible! Maybe the heat produced a mental block, but I was quite content with the memory lapse.

Psalm 103 talks about a memory lapse too, and it is very deliberate. Verse 12 says, "...as far as the east is from the west, so far has he removed our transgressions from us." God totally blocks out our sin, once we have accepted the sacrifice of His Son, Jesus. No matter what we have done, if we have acknowledged our need for the forgiveness of Christ, we are forgiven. 2 Corinthians 5:17 says, "Therefore, if anyone is in Christ, he is a new creation; the old has gone, the new has come!"

Being in Christ is like perpetual spring - life is fresh

and new, colorful and full of promise. There is no fear of on-coming winter, no dread. We are free to enjoy life to the fullest. Newness in Christ is possible for us all.

****

Once Again

There's a song by Matt Redman that says - "Once again I look upon the cross where You died. I'm humbled by Your mercy and I'm broken inside. Once again I thank You, once again I pour out my life."

While in Israel we visited a heritage village. It was much like the heritage villages here in North America that portray past history in tableau, with real actors and working artifacts. This village was in Nazareth and was laid out to represent the town as it would have been in the time of Jesus.

The day we visited, it was raining - pouring rain, in fact - so we were the only people there. Most of the actors seemed to be keeping inside the small shelters, which didn't really keep them dry because the roofs were made of thatch and far from water-proof. We moved from one scene to the next - the potter's, the weaver's, the wine press, and finally the carpenter's shop. It was here the fact that this was a representation of Jesus' home hit me. I looked at the tools, the kind of rough wood he would have worked with, and Jesus became more real to me.

Perhaps that's why the tableau we saw next had such an impact. The figure at the centre was made of rough wood too, and was draped with a simple cloth. The lighting was subdued, flickering with small oil lamps, their tiny flames leaning toward the focal point of the display. The cross. The cross of Christ.

As the song says, once again I was struck by what Jesus suffered, what He endured for me. I was struck not just by the physical pain He was subjected to, but by the torture of having the sin of the world put upon His shoulders, the agony of knowing His Father was turning His face away.

And once again I became aware that there is nothing I can do to make it up to Him. No remorse, no penance, no acts of kindness. Nothing I do can repay that debt. And once again that act of pure mercy stunned me. The unconditional gift of love and forgiveness caused my heart to break. And that, I realized once again, is the only thing Jesus wants of me. A heart broken wide enough for Him to enter in.

Thousands all over the world recognize that act of mercy and love - the death of Jesus on that cross. I pray that thousands of hearts will break wide enough.

"So they took Jesus and led him away. Carrying the cross by himself, Jesus went to the place called Skull

Hill (in Hebrew, Golgotha). There they crucified him"
(John 19:16-18, NLT).

****

Sea Shells and the Process of Faith

Picture three little girls, their blonde heads bent
down as they walk along the seashore. Beach combing
was one of our favorite things to do when we were in
Papua New Guinea. The shells were numerous and
almost all of them beautiful. My daughters and I spent
quite some time walking the white sand and usually
went home with pails full of treasures.

But we had been cautioned to be careful. Certain
kinds of shells contained a creature that was deadly.
Tourists who weren't in the know had died because of
them. We had to learn which were safe and which
were not. We had to learn that some things, even
though they look beautiful, can be dangerous. As I
watched my daughters pick the shells from the sand, I
was thankful for the warnings we had received,
thankful that we could rely on the wisdom of those
who knew the dangers.

In the same way, we sometimes have to be careful
about spiritual things in our lives. We have to
understand that not everything that looks and sounds
good is true or even of benefit. It's easy to get drawn

into something that appears wholesome, appears right, but is a concoction of deceit. The writer of the book of Proverbs knew this when he wrote, "There is a way that seems right to a man, but in the end it leads to death" (Prov. 14:12).

The Apostle John also warned us to be careful, when he said, "Dear friends, do not believe every spirit, but test the spirits to see whether they are from God, because many false prophets have gone out into the world" (1John 4:1).

God has given us ways to discover the truth and He has promised that if we seek Him with all our heart, mind and soul, we will find Him. The key seems to be that we never stop. If we sit back, thinking we know all there is to know about Him, we are in danger of arrogance and self-deceit. Finding and knowing God is not just an event in time. Faith is a process and a lifestyle that produces fruit.

A wise person once said, "No-one has the complete truth but God Himself." I think that's why it's so vital to get to know Him, to depend on His wisdom, to lean only on His strength. In this thin slice of time we call our life, we are far too limited to assume we know it all. So it's wise to heed the writers of scripture when they tell us to be careful. It's wise to heed the words God inspired, to gain His wisdom. It's wise to agree that we are frail humans and only God is God.

****

Restoration in Montreal

I was raised with all the tenets of The Church, and tried to do all the right things, say all the right prayers, keep all the right ordinances. I left it, convinced I just wasn't good enough for God. Then one day all that I thought was safe and secure crumbled when I tried to reach for it.

My husband sought the answers first, and in seeking them found more questions, but also found the God of his childhood. I was afraid to look again. Afraid He still wouldn't let me find Him. But I took a risk one day, overlooking the Stewart River in the Yukon, and asked Him to show Himself. He did and my heart melted as I moved into a culture of faith, a community of believers.

As I learned the truth in His word, I became angry at The Church of my childhood. They'd lied to me. So I thought. It was easy to lay the blame at the foot of that altar.

Flash forward twenty years or so - I was holding the portfolio of Communications for our church's association. They paid my way to Montreal for a conference and I found myself in a nunnery. Once housing seven hundred women of God, it was reduced to hotel status with a small wing left for the aged Sisters of Charity still in residence. I passed the statues of the Virgin on my way to breakfast, glanced sidelong at the portraits of Christ pointing to his heart, exposed. I smiled and said "Bon matins," to the nuns.

Then one night we were invited to go to the Notre Dame Cathedral at the heart of the old city to see a "light show." We sat in the old pews, heard a lecturer describe the building of the Cathedral as portions of it were lit around us. The sculpture, the art, the richness of history, and yes, of faith, amazed me. But when the screen we'd been watching suddenly folded back to reveal the altar, my heart almost stopped. It gleamed, shone, soared toward the heavens, and in the silence forced our eyes to look up. Look up and behold our God.

Our host announced we were welcome to draw near for a closer look. As we walked toward the altar, I kept my eyes raised until we were standing directly in front of it. Then I saw The Lamb.

Carved in bas relief, He sat on the throne with the multitudes around Him. Angels covering their faces with their wings, angels hovering above and around, saints throwing down their crowns, saints bowing. The multitude worshiping. And at the centre, The Lamb.

And I wept there, in that cathedral. I wept because He had chosen to reveal Himself to me in a place where I was convinced He could not be found. He restored my heritage to me, its richness, its beauty, and its essential truth. At the centre, The Lamb.

I wept there, because some day that's where we will

be, worshipping at His feet. The Apostle John described it in the last book of the Bible, Revelation - "Then I looked and heard the voice of many angels, numbering thousands upon thousands, and ten thousand times ten thousand. They encircled the throne and the living creatures and the elders. In a loud voice they sang: "Worthy is the Lamb, who was slain, to receive power and wealth and wisdom and strength and honor and glory and praise!" Then I heard every creature in heaven and on earth and under the earth and on the sea, and all that is in them, singing: "To him who sits on the throne and to the Lamb be praise and honor and glory and power, for ever and ever!" (Revelation 5:11-13).

Amen!

****

One Year in Paradise

It wasn't until we landed on the airstrip at Port Moresby, Papua New Guinea, and stepped out into the humid heat, that I first asked myself, "What on earth have we done?" It had taken me and my family 26 hours to fly from Vancouver, Canada, north towards the top of the globe, down the coast of Russia, China and Japan to this South Pacific island just north of Australia. We had driven through a blizzard to reach Vancouver, and knew the shock of arriving in the tropics would be great. It began to dawn as we stood under slow-moving fans in the long line at the customs counter, aware that we were the only "whiteskins" with perspiration dripping off our noses

With our passports and visas checked, we made our way to the waiting area, tried to find a seat directly under a fan and bemoaned the fact that we hadn't yet changed our Canadian "loonies" into PNG kina, making the Coke$_l$ machine inaccessible.

People-watching helped pass the time. Women stood and squatted in the lines, many in national dress, the bright "meriblaus," a full top extending almost to the knees and "lap-lap," an ankle-length piece of cloth wrapped around twice and tied at the waist. Many bore facial tattoos, blue lines and dots on their foreheads and cheeks. Almost all of them had children on their laps and at their knees. The men were mostly small-built, all wearing shorts and T-shirts, some bearded and a couple with matted hair braided and tied at the back of the neck. Almost no-one wore shoes.

The noise in the room was considerable. If my ear had been able to distinguish at the time, I probably would have picked out several languages, (there are

869, at last count, in a country roughly the size of Alberta). I was having trouble just trying to understand the common trade language, Melanesian Pidgin, which blared over a loudspeaker whenever a flight was ready to board. The national folk didn't seem to have the same problem as they surged toward the exit at each announcement, leaving emptied seats snatched up by those sitting and squatting on the floor.

Two long hours later we boarded our Air Niugini flight to the other side of the island where we would go to "jungle camp," the orientation spot for short term workers in the country. The shock of arrival continued as we flew over the lush landscape, but it slowly gave way to wonder at the beauty of P.N.G. The coast-line is quickly enveloped in jungle and Sago swamps (Sago palms provide the staple food, even though they have six inch thorns surrounding their trunks). The swamps are bordered by a ridge of mountains running like a spine through the island.

Our small plane bounced as we neared the high ridges but we ignored the instability and peered down at clusters of village huts and gardens cut into steep slopes. The land descended quickly as we approached the city of Madang, clinging to the edge of coral reefs in the clear waters of the Bismark Sea. The airport in Madang is a smaller version of Port Moresby, minus the fans. It was at this point we realized that, although we were visitors in this country, we would not be tourists. We had come to work at a centre called the Summer Institute of Linguistics, (S.I.L.).

The S.I.L. worker who met us in Madang, ushered us to our "taxi," a one-ton truck with long wooden benches down the sides and middle, covered by a steel frame and canvass tarp rolled up on both sides. We, and another family, loaded our considerable gear into it and clung to the metal frame as we lurched up a narrow trail toward the site of the Pacific Orientation Course (POC). For those of us without fear of heights, the view was breathtaking. The rest preferred to admire the banana and coconut trees on the mountain side.

At POC, we were met by "wantoks" – a PNG term meaning countrymen, those who speak the same language. It was wonderful to see those smiling Canadian faces. They introduced us to life at "jungle camp." Our accommodations consisted of one room divided by a plywood wall with two mosquito-screened bunks on one side and a double bed on the other. Showers were around back, made out of a bucket on a pulley and sporadically heated by a wood stove. We quickly learned to give the bucket a whack before using it, to dislodge the geckos and spiders.

Meals were taken communally with eight other families in residence, all of us assigned to work together to help prepare and cook the food on a huge wood stove. Often it was a challenge to guess what we would be served at the next meal. On one occasion we were told we were eating "Sepik chicken." After we had taken a few bites, the cook explained the Sepik is one of the country's largest rivers and the "chickens" have thick leathery skins and large teeth. We were savoring crocodile tail. It wasn't until a few months later that we were offered another traditional delicacy, roasted sago grubs. As I accepted the skewered grubs, blackened by an open cooking fire, I was thankful for the "jungle camp" experience and pretended I really didn't know what I was popping into my mouth.

Our days at P.O.C. were filled with lectures on the culture and customs, covering such things as the common practice of holding hands or linking "pinkies" (your smallest finger) as you chat with a member of the same sex, and taboos like stepping over food, even though it may be scattered on the ground. Language learning (Melanesian Pidgin), taught by a young Dutch woman and a Papua New Guinean man, also took up many hours as we practiced dialogues and concentrated on grammatical construction. The rest of our time was spent swimming and snorkeling in the ocean and hiking in the tropical heat. By the end of the two weeks we were feeling much more comfortable with all of the above and felt confident, as, our orientation over, we boarded an S.I.L. plane for the short hop over the mountains to Ukarumpa. The highlands town is S.I.L.'s main centre housing about 450 translators, literacy workers and support personnel.

In spite of our time at P.O.C., culture shock continued in Ukarumpa. We had to adjust to meeting people with every kind of accent, from Swiss to Korean, hearing broad banana leaves clapping in the wind one minute and the sighing of pine trees the next, shopping in the open market and remembering to always carry an umbrella for protection against sun as well as rain. The first morning I approached the market I heard a loud voice and my heart skipped a beat or two. As I got closer I was able to make out words like "Bikpela God" and realized someone was preaching. Everyone listened attentively and bowed their heads in prayer when he finished, declaring the market open. I said a quick prayer myself, before milling among the people, being careful not to step over any food or touch anything before I bought it, two of the taboos we had learned at jungle camp. I was extremely grateful for the Pidgin classes at P.O.C., which enabled me at least to ask, "Em wannem samting?" (What is this?) and "Em i hamas?" (How much?) It was obvious, however, that the people spoke Pidgin at a more rapid rate and with a different inflection than the Dutch teacher who taught us the grammar.

As the days stretched into weeks, activities like going

to market became routine. I managed to engage in a bit of intelligible Pidgin conversation and gradually began to relax. I discovered many of the people came to the market from faraway villages, often waking at 4 in the morning to walk the distance to Ukarumpa in time. Then they travel the seven kilometers by PMV (public motor vehicle), which could be anything from a jeep to a broken down bus or even a dump truck, to the nearest town, Kainantu, where they would continue to sell their produce.

Kainantu is a conglomeration of tin buildings and clapboard houses, its streets crowded, especially on fortnight Fridays (payday) with Bouai-chewing men. (Bouai is a beetle nut that turns saliva blood red). Swarms of chickens, kids and even the odd pig or two share the road and boardwalks with wary women. The women carry their vegetables, fruits and even babies in bilums, (brightly coloured string bags they weave themselves), placing the long woven strap on their heads, the heavy bag resting on their backs. It's common to see a woman carrying fifty to seventy-five pounds, or more, often with a small child on her shoulders or hip as well.

The men carry artifacts. Their basketry is beautiful, as is their carving on bamboo. There are always bows and arrows to be had, as well as black-stained pukpuks (carved crocodiles) with cowrie shell eyes. Eventually I was able to buy a well used Kundu - a tall hour-glass shaped drum carved out of wood with a snake or animal skin bound with vines on one end. I'd seen the Kundu used often at the Sing-sings – a raucous festival-like event where people gather from miles around in full regalia of feathers and paint to dance the stories and rituals of their lives.

As my language skills increased, so did my appreciation for the highlands people.   Though they were at first reserved and unsure, I was able to establish relationships. The women are remarkable for their strength, not only of body but also of spirit, bearing hardships with both stamina and an unquenchable hope. These qualities have stood them in good stead in a society that is unpredictable, often violent, in a country where the infant mortality rate is more than 50% and adult life expectancy is relatively short. Their lives are hard but their souls are not embittered.

In that one year in Papua New Guinea we were privileged to be part of a process that is having a positive impact. We met children and adults who are learning to read and write in their own language, because of S.I.L.'s efforts. We spoke with young people who have hope of attending one of the country's few high schools. We saw healthy children and knew the medical assistance was making a life and death difference. In a world full of tragedy and heartbreaking despair, our year in Papua New Guinea was a year of realizing there is hope, a hope kept alive by people who truly believe "greater love has no one than this, that one lay down his life for his friends."

####

If you have enjoyed A Traveler's Advisory, please consider posting a review of this book on Amazon and any other places you deem appropriate. Thank You!

ABOUT THE AUTHOR

Marcia Lee Laycock is an award-winning writer and speaker. She has written a regular devotional column for over 20 years and has five books in print as well as several ebooks, available through Helping Hands Press, Small Pond Press, Amazon and on her website.

To sign up to receive Marcia's regular emailed devotionals, or to book her for a speaking engagement, contact her at marcialeelaycock@gmail.com

www.marcialeelaycock.com

www.smallpondpress.com

Made in the USA
Charleston, SC
04 January 2016